JACOBITE LEGACY

Prince Charles Edward Stuart.
A miniature after Sir Robert Strange.

JACOBITE LEGACY

A CATALOGUE OF MEMORABILIA OF THE JACOBITE ERA

DR MARTIN KELVIN
FSA (SCOT)

Published by
G C Book Publishers Ltd
7 South Main Street,
Wigtown
Scotland
DG8 9EH

First published November 2003

ISBN 1 872350 68 2

Copyright 2003 Martin Kelvin

Martin Kelvin asserts his right under the Copyright, Designs and Patents Act 1988 to be identified as the author of this work.

Printed under the supervision of
MRM Graphics Ltd, Winslow, Bucks

For Matthew and Lizzie

Specialist photography
by
Andy Kelvin.

FOREWORD

Some years ago, the late and well-loved Scottish historian Fitzroy Maclean, was in the process of examining some family documents, when he came across a scrap of neatly folded paper. On opening it, he discovered a tiny miniature drawing of Bonnie Prince Charlie, and the written text: "Prince Charles Edward 1745 - given to my Grandfather's care by another Jacobite gentleman who was afraid to have the portrait found on him". Sir Fitzroy goes on to describe his sense of wonderment and fascination at the discovery of this thrilling link with the past, sensations shared with other, earlier authors, noted for their expertise in the field of Jacobite history. Robert Chambers, Grant Francis, Andrew Lang and Donald Nicholas, were all avid collectors of Jacobite memorabilia, and those of us professing an interest in the subject to this day, are equally familiar with the sensations evoked in Sir Fitzroy by the discovery of the precious drawing. The objects of Jacobite material culture are a visible as well as a tangible link with a brief, exciting, and in many ways tragic period of Scottish history, providing a bridge for the enthusiast to his Jacobite heritage.

* * * * *

LIST OF ILLUSTRATIONS
Between pages 80 & 81

Frontispiece: Miniature of Prince Charles Edward Stuart.

1. Gold and agate snuffbox..i.
2. Interior of upper lid with inscription.....................................i.
3. Mackinnon belt buckle..ii.
4. Crown seal with a likeness of the Prince after Strange......... iii.
5. Wax impression of above..iii.
6. Traquair watch fob seal..iv.
7. Detail of above..iv.
8. Portrait of the Prince after Hussey......................................v.
9. Hair ring containing a sheaf of the Prince's hair....................iv.
10. Memorial ring to Flora Macdonald...................................vi.
11. Crown brooch inscribed "Do Come"...............................vi.
12. Obverse side of brooch..vi.
13. Jacobite medals 1712-88..vii.
14. Anti-Jacobite medals 1717-46...vii.
15. Miniature of James VIII after Alexis Belle......................viii.
16. Snuffmull belonging to William Hamilton of Bangour..........viii.
17. Snuffmull belonging to Alexander Smith of Longmay.........ix.
18. Lid, showing inscription..ix.
19. Jacobite ribbon...x.
20. Glass medallion depicting James VIII..............................x.
21. Silver "Amor et Spes" medal...x.
22. Sea Serjeants seal ring..xi.
23. Jacobite seal ring, "Turno Tempus Erit".........................xi.
24. Seal ring adorned with Jacobite rose and singlebud............xi.
25. Jacobite powderhorn dated 1716....................................xii.
26. Close-up of inscription...xii.

27. Engraving of Jenny Cameron of Glendessary....................xiii.
28. Engraving of the Battle of Culloden by Laurie & Whittle...xiv.
29. Watch fob seal engraved "Redii".......................................xiv.
30. Engraving of Charles by Armytage.....................................xv.
31. Watch fob seal engraved "Awa Whigs Awa"......................xv.
32. Seal ring engraved "Dinna Forget"...................................xvi.
33. Engraving of Prince Charles Edward by Edelinck.............xvi.

CONTENTS

I. INTRODUCTION........................Page 14

II. HISTORY......................................Page 19

III. JACOBITE MEMORABILIA.......Page 26

IV. KEY..Page 31

V. CATALOGUE................................Page 35

A Jacobite Legacy

INTRODUCTION

A large number of artefacts or memorabilia has passed down to the present generation from Jacobite times. Many are connected in some way with the Rising of 1745, but others go back even further, to the very beginnings of the Jacobite period, in 1688. There is such a tremendous variety of these objects, that, arising from an intense fascination in that era, the author has created a dictionary or catalogue, designed to define these objects specifically, together with brief explanatory notes where required. There can be many reasons for the inclusion of specific objects in a list of this kind. They may have belonged originally to a known Jacobite, or even to Prince Charles or James III himself, or some other member of the Stuart royal family. They may, on the contrary, have been in the possession of a Hanoverian soldier, possibly even of the Duke of Cumberland himself. Such objects would be anti-Jacobite, but despite this, they merit inclusion in a list of items associated with the Jacobite movement. Possibly the particular article was found on a Jacobite battlefield, for example, a spur, or perhaps a musket or cannonball, and this, too, would constitute an item of Jacobite memorabilia.

The provenance attaching to these memorabilia is frequently sketchy and unreliable. The enthusiastic collector, confronted with items of such rarity, is apt to allow himself to be carried away by his eagerness to acquire the desired objects, but despite this he should at all times try to maintain a healthy scepticism, since provenance, in its true sense, seldom exists. Where an object purports to be of Jacobite significance, and has been passed down through successive generations of the same family, then this is probably the best provenance anyone is likely to obtain. Our

A Jacobite Legacy

cannonball, picked up, we are told, on the battlefield of Culloden, is just like any other cannonball, and no-one can either confirm this or deny it. It might be a perfectly genuine Jacobite artefact, but equally, it might not. Tradition in a family regarding a particular object does go some way towards proof, for example, if a particular family has farmed the land on which the battlefield lay, and the cannonball was said to have been passed down through the generations, this might be considered as partly establishing some kind of provenance. On the other hand, a silver band round the cannonball, engraved with an inscription recounting its history, might establish provenance for some, whilst the more sceptical might claim the object to be suspect, the presence of the silver ring together with an apparently authentic inscription merely imparting added cachet to a relatively commonplace object. Labels were often attached to such items at a much later date, but this does not imply that the object is not genuine, and the older the style of writing, the less likely it is to be spurious.

Where certain objects have been, and perhaps still are, in the possession of a family with Jacobite ancestry, is no guarantee that this has always been the case. The Victorians were great collectors, and existing Jacobite collections could have been, and often were, added to by subsequent generations. In the mid-18th century, the giving of mementos or souvenirs was widely practised. Charles Edward cut off many pieces of his tartan plaid to present as gifts to those who had helped him escape, and the practice of cutting off locks of hair was followed throughout the century. Locks of Clementina's and James' hair were presented to eager recipients, and even the infant Charles and his brother Henry had their locks clipped to send to Stuart supporters. The sceptical have suggested that if all the hair Charles had supplied to his adherents was gathered together, it would fill an entire room, but judging from the number of such items, and the miniscule amount of hair required to fit a ring

A Jacobite Legacy

or brooch, a fistful would probably be nearer the truth. Bonnie Prince Charlie was said to have left his bonnet at Moy Hall when he had to leave hurriedly in the early hours of February 17th, 1746, during the Rout of Moy, and this bonnet is preserved at the Hall. However, another, similar, bonnet is in existence, which is also said to be the very one left there by the Prince! Medals, either Jacobite or anti-Jacobite, might appear to be clear evidence of provenance in themselves, but it must be remembered that such items are relatively easy to fake, and it is known that a few have been fabricated from the original moulds, although the quality may have suffered, resulting from the deterioration of the old moulds due to rusting. During the first quarter of the 19th century, Matthew Young produced copies in this way, sometimes incorrectly matching the obverse and reverse of particular medals, and the collector should be aware of these "mismatches". Miniatures and paintings, although far less likely to be deliberate fakes, were sometimes painted by Victorian artists, seeking to depict the romantic and nostalgic elements of the Jacobite era. Likenesses of Charles and other prominent Jacobites produced during this period, although eminently collectible in their own right, could be confused by the unwary with the work of contemporary 18th century artists.

The ultimate fate of some of the personal possessions of the exiled Stuart royal family is of great interest to Jacobite enthusiasts. When Charles Edward Stuart died in 1788, he left all his goods and effects, which included the Polish crown jewels which had belonged to his mother, Clementina Sobieska, to Charlotte, his daughter by Clementina Walkinshaw. Although he had not corresponded with her throughout her lifetime, he became reconciled to her, finally legitimising her birth, and it was she who took care of him during the remaining four years of his life, as his health began to decline. Charlotte herself died the following year, and left all her possessions to Henry, Cardinal York, directing that,

A Jacobite Legacy

apart from items of jewellery specifically mentioned in her will, the remaining valuables should be sold, in order to fund the pensions which she had bequeathed to her mother and several members of her household. Of the vast amount of private correspondence and other documents accumulated by the Stuarts in their exile, a significant quantity had been removed to the Palazzo San Clemente in Florence, and this portion Charlotte bequeathed to the Abbé Waters. The remaining papers, kept in the Muti Palace and comprising the greater amount, had come into Henry's possession on the death of his brother in 1788. These two important archives were eventually purchased by the Prince Regent, and so finally reunited nearly 30 years after Charles' death, although some papers had been privately removed and sold, and others destroyed through hard usage and neglect. The entire archive, comprising the 541 volumes of the Stuart Papers, is in the ownership of Her Majesty the Queen, and held in the Archive Room at Windsor Castle, while a further collection, comprising a number of those papers sold privately, are now in the British Library.

Henry Benedict, Cardinal York, Bishop of Frascati, was a man of considerable wealth, but after the invasion of the French army, he had to flee his magnificent palace, seeking refuge at Venice, where he sold most of his jewels, it is said, in order to give financial assistance to the Pope, and so prevent the sack of the Vatican. Amongst the jewels sold, was an enormous sapphire surrounded by sixteen diamonds. This jewel was brought by devious means to the Prince Regent, who gave it to his daughter Princess Charlotte. Henry survived his brother 19 years, and on his death, bequeathed the ruby ring which had belonged to King Charles I, as well as the Badge of the Order of the Thistle which Charles Edward had worn, and which contained a hidden portrait of his wife, Princess Louise of Stolberg, to the Prince Regent, later George IV. Along with a Garter jewel, these now form part of the Scottish Regalia, and are housed in Edinburgh Castle.

A Jacobite Legacy

The most magnificent of all Jacobite artefacts, must be the incredible gold caddinet which Henry had made for himself to celebrate his new status as Henry IX, beside which even the silver-gilt canteen of cutlery made by the Jacobite goldsmith, Ebenezer Oliphant, which was recovered from Charles Edward's baggage after Culloden, pales into unlikely insignificance. Perhaps this was one of the items sold by Henry at Venice, and did his orb-shaped buttons of rock crystal share the same fate? We can only conjecture about the previous history of such items as these, or of Henry's mitre, in which the sapphire referred to above once glistened, or of his perfume bottle, which has somehow managed to survive in pristine condition after nearly two hundred years.

As with all other artefacts, but particularly with objects of this kind and rarity, it will be for the individual to draw his or her own conclusions regarding provenance, from a careful study of the object, having regard to any history attaching to it. It should always be remembered too, that merely because a reliable provenance is absent, does not necessarily indicate that a particular object is a fake. The absence may be worrying, but it could have been lost for a variety of reasons, and, once lost, there is no way that it can ever be reinstated. Labels may become detached, and in the absence of a verbal history passed on from one generation to the next, posterity is permanently denied an integral part of its history. Despite all this, and with the words "caveat emptor" ringing in our ears, it has to be stated that few thrills match that attained by the collector holding in his hands for the very first time an object which is, he has satisfied himself, of Jacobite significance.

* * * * *

A Jacobite Legacy

THE HISTORY OF THE JACOBITE MOVEMENT

When Charles II died in 1685, he was succeeded by his brother James, who became King James VII of Scotland, and II of England. James had converted to Catholicism several years before, and was determined to ease the many restrictions placed at that time on its adherents. This angered both his English and Scottish subjects, but when in 1688 James' second wife, Mary Beatrice of Modena, gave birth to a son, thereby ensuring the Catholic succession, an invitation was issued to the Protestant Prince William of Orange, married to Mary, James' daughter by his first wife, Ann Hyde, to accept the throne. William eagerly accepted the invitation, and duly landed at Torbay in Devonshire, at the head of an army of 14000 Protestant mercenaries. James assembled an army of highland clansmen, and the Jacobite movement, whose adherents were predominantly Catholic or Episcopalian, was born. The opposing armies met at the Pass of Killiecrankie in 1689, and in the ensuing battle the highlanders were victorious, although their charismatic leader, John Graham of Claverhouse, known to his followers as Bonnie Dundee, was killed. The Jacobite army, named for Jacobus, the Latin form of James, then attempted to take possession of the town of Dunkeld, held by a small force of Cameronians, but, being unaccustomed to street fighting, failed miserably to do so, and retired dispirited to their homes, along with the considerable booty taken at Killiecrankie. His army having literally vanished before his eyes, James and his family were forced to flee to France, where they were given succour by Louis XIV at the old palace of St Germain-en-Laye. The following year a huge army composed mainly of Irish Catholics was defeated by King William III at the Battle of the Boyne, thus ending James' aspirations of regaining his lost throne.

James VII died in 1701, and in 1708, the year following the

A Jacobite Legacy

Treaty of Union between Scotland and England, his son James Francis Edward Stuart, known as the Old Pretender, at the head of a small French fleet, and accompanied by an equally small army, attempted to make a landing in Scotland, but were sighted near the Isle of May by the British fleet. A naval engagement followed, during which one French warship was destroyed, and the others returned in haste to France, along with the disconsolate James, whose long and sad features had earned him the sobriquet "Old Mr Melancholy". Four years later, in 1712, James and his younger sister, Princess Louisa, contracted smallpox, and although he himself made a full recovery, his sister unfortunately died.

In 1715, a further attempt was made to regain the throne for the Stuarts, when a large army was assembled by the Earl of Mar, on the pretext of a hunting expedition in the Braes of Mar. The government forces, whose numbers were much inferior, were led by the Duke of Argyll, yet fought so well at the Battle of Sheriffmuir, near Dunblane, that each side was able to claim the victory. Stuart hopes were dashed once more when a Scottish army led by Mackintosh of Borlum surrendered to government forces at Preston.

Four years later, in 1719, an expedition launched with Spanish help was again doomed to failure. The plan had been to combine a major attack in the west of England with a much smaller one in Scotland. A small force duly landed at Loch Alsh, in Kintail, but the main body of troops failed to make a landing when their fleet was dispersed in a severe storm. The tiny army of Spaniards was forced to surrender after their defeat at the Battle of Glenshiel. James, by this time, was living at the Palazzo Muti in Rome, which had been provided for him by the Pope, who in addition supplied him with a pension sufficient, with careful management, to maintain himself and his somewhat extended family. His entourage was not inconsiderable, and amongst them were several of the clan chiefs,

A Jacobite Legacy

who had fought for him during the 1715 Rebellion, and who, being exiled under the Act of Attainder, had severe practical difficulties in raising the rents on their estates, and were therefore, for the most part, financially dependent on him. At the same time he was constantly in receipt of requests for pecuniary assistance from Jacobites who had lost everything in the Stuart cause, most of them very deserving, and so life in the Jacobite court was not an easy one, and its courtiers were in many respects leading a hand to mouth existence, while at the same time, spies reported in detail the minutiae of court life in Rome to the Hanoverian government.

In 1719, James had married the Polish princess, Maria Clementina Sobieska, after her dramatic rescue from imprisonment in Austria, where she had been confined at the instigation of the British whilst en route to the wedding. On 31st December, 1720, his son Charles Edward, Prince of Wales, was born, followed five years later by the birth of a second son, Henry Benedict, Duke of York. Clementina was a spirited young lady, who felt oppressed by the dull, staid, atmosphere at the Jacobite court. In 1725, after a series of domestic arguments, she sought refuge in a convent, remaining for two years. On her return at last to the Palazzo Muti, she devoted herself more and more to religious contemplation, but her health declined, and she died in 1735, at the early age of 33.

In 1743, the French decided to finance a further effort to restore the Stuarts to their throne, having satisfied themselves that there was likely to be a considerable body of support both from the English Jacobites as well as the loyal clans. A large fleet was assembled in 1744, but before it could depart, a storm blew up which wrecked many of the ships still in port, and the remainder were scattered by the English navy, whose spies had made them aware of French plans. Charles Edward, who had been asked by the French to lead the expedition, now waited at Dunkirk to receive

A Jacobite Legacy

the news of a renewed "descent" on Scotland, but as time passed, he became increasingly aware that the French harboured no such intentions, and it was suggested that they had simply been using the Stuarts to divert English troops from Flanders, where they were presently engaged in a war against the French. It was at this point that Charles conceived the idea of making the attempt to restore his father's throne without enlisting French aid at the outset, believing that, once he had the full support of the clans, the French would be morally obliged to assist him with arms and men. Accordingly, he set about equipping two privateers, and filling them with arms, including guns, broadswords, and cannon, although it seems likely that the French were not unaware of these preparations.

His landing, on July 23rd (old style) 1745, was an inauspicious one, the attempt outrageously audacious, and yet it must be conceded that Charles came within an ace of succeeding. He had the ablest of generals in Lord George Murray, yet under the influence of his Irish senior officers, held him in constant suspicion, and seldom took his advice. Charles, also referred to as the Young Pretender, (from the French "prétendant" = "claimant") erected his standard on a knoll above the river Finnan at the head of Loch Shiel, and with his small army, marched eastwards, taking the town of Perth and entering the capital. His early victory against General Sir John Cope at Prestonpans was followed by great celebrations amongst the Jacobites at Edinburgh, before the disastrous march south to Derby and the final retreat to Scotland, under threat from three opposing armies. Support from the English Jacobites had failed to materialise, and the supposedly large Welsh contingent set off too late to be of any assistance. Despite gaining a victory over the Hanoverian army at Falkirk Muir, unconfirmed reports of widescale desertion amongst the clansmen led its leaders to advise a retreat to the north, thus denying themselves access to the east coast ports vital to their supply links with France, and so rendering their ultimate defeat inevitable.

A Jacobite Legacy

Charles' mistrust of Lord George was now to prove most fateful, at Culloden, the final battle of the Forty-Five rebellion, a battle which should never have been fought, over ground entirely unsuited to the highlanders' only battle tactic, the highland charge, the army itself exhausted, starving, and reduced to only half its full strength. The Duke of Cumberland, at the head of 9000 men, Redcoats as well as "loyal" clans, and supported by a considerable train of artillery, easily defeated an army of half its size, putting in excess of 1000 men to the sword, and thereafter treating the wounded and dying with such brutality, that he was ever after referred to as "Butcher" Cumberland. The remnants of the shattered highland army met briefly at Ruthven in Badenoch, before dispersing, each man seeking his own escape, as advised by the Prince himself, "as best he could".

Following the defeat of the clans, the massive and brutal recriminations in the highlands began, with the proscription of highland dress, and the Disarming Act that were to follow. The houses of the Jacobite lairds were put to the torch, and their estates forfeited. Many of the leading Jacobites were found guilty of treason, and were put to death on the scaffold, whilst large numbers were transported to the Colonies. Some were freed in 1747 under the Act of Indemnity, but many of those who escaped after Culloden would never be permitted to return to their homeland, and would lead a life of poverty in exile. Many of those awaiting trial in the overcrowded gaols or prison hulks died of disease, starvation, or ill treatment. The Prince himself spent five months in hiding, a reward of £30,000 on his head, assisted not only by a small retinue of faithful followers, but by many others who had not joined his standard, despite their Jacobite sympathies. His rescue from Loch nan Uamh on 20 September 1746 by a French frigate at the sixth attempt, might be seen as more than merely fortuitous, since it conveniently saved the government the embarrassment of a trial and its unsavoury consequences.

A Jacobite Legacy

Charles, after a few months spent in a fruitless attempt to secure French aid for yet another "descent", settled down to a life dominated by alcohol dependence, intrigue, and fear of assassination, travelling from country to country, often in disguise, and under a variety of aliases. When Prince Henry took holy orders in 1747, Charles was devastated. The Treaty of Aix-la-Chapelle between France and Great Britain was ratified the following year, but Charles, whose presence in Paris had become an embarrassment, refused to leave, and had to be forcibly expelled from the country.

In the ensuing years, several plots against the Hanoverians were perpetrated, and during at least one of these, probably more, he visited London, and in 1750 is known to have attended a meeting of the Oak Society, a Jacobite organisation which met at the Crown and Anchor tavern in the Strand. This visit was known to King George II, who took no action against him. Charles lived for some years with his mistress, Clementina Walkinshaw, whom he had met at Bannockburn during the Rising of 1745, and who bore him a child, Charlotte. When James VIII died in 1766, Charles had not seen him since his departure for France twenty-three years before, and the Pope refused to recognise his Royal title. Charles spent much of his time at the Palazzo Muti, where his father had held court for so long, but his behaviour became more and more antisocial, and he succeeded in alienating many of his most loyal followers. At length he was persuaded, on the promise of a pension from Louis XV, to take a wife, and, hopefully, to produce an heir, and in 1772 he married the young Princess Louise of Stolberg. The marriage was not a happy one, and she left him after some years for the Italian poet, Count Alfieri.

In 1784 Charles became reconciled to his daughter Charlotte, whom he had seen only once since her childhood, her

A Jacobite Legacy

mother having taken her into a convent at that time, in order to escape his violent outbursts. Charles and Louise had been living in Florence at the Palazzo San Clemente, and he now introduced Charlotte to Florentine society as the Duchess of Albany, having legitimised her birth. His health in decline, Charles and his daughter took up residence in the Muti Palace, and Charlotte was fêted once more, this time by Roman society, a rôle which she and Charles both relished. Charlotte had cared for her father throughout the period of their reconciliation, and when in January 1788 he had a stroke, leaving him paralysed, she continued to minister to him until his death, some two weeks later. His brother, Henry Benedict, Cardinal York, ordered a medal to be struck in his honour, and assumed his Royal titles. Charlotte herself died the following year, leaving all her effects, formerly belonging to Charles, to his brother Henry. She, in obedience to Charles' wishes, had not married, but was mistress to the Prince de Rohan, Archbishop of Bordeaux, by whom she had three children. Henry died in 1807, at the age of 82, by which time however, the Hanoverian dynasty had become fully established, and the prospect of a Stuart restoration had disappeared forever.

* * * * *

A Jacobite Legacy

JACOBITE MEMORABILIA

Most Jacobite sentimentalism is centred on the Rebellion of 1745. Although the Jacobite movement had begun some 57 years earlier, matters came to a dramatic head following the events of that year. It is true to say that the vast majority of artefacts of the Jacobite era are related in some way to that brief episode of Scottish history, and this is reflected in the treatment given to this subject in the chapter devoted to the history of the Jacobite movement.

Although Jacobite hopes were virtually extinguished after the death of Prince Charles Edward Stuart, nevertheless Jacobite sentiment persisted. The closet English Jacobites, dutifully accepting the God-given heritable rights demanded by the Stuart dynasty, were quite content to drink their clandestine toasts to the "King over the Water", but were not prepared to translate their love of the Stuarts into physical action. This is hardly surprising, since few of the English gentry were trained in the art of war, and could not rely, as did the Scottish lairds, on a large body of retainers, all of whom were habitually skilled in the use of arms. Even some of the Lowland lairds, including the Earl of Kilmarnock and John Murray of Broughton, could not bring more than a single man into the field. Charles himself probably did not expect any significant English rising before the arrival of the 15,000 troops prevented, more probably by a lack of commitment on the part of the French government rather than the adverse weather conditions often implicated, from leaving their shores.

With the passage of the Jacobite threat, those adherents to the Stuart cause did not abandon their Jacobite sympathies overnight, but continued to nurture sentiment which was both pro-Stuart and anti-Whig. Jacobite secret societies proliferated throughout both Scotland and England. In Scotland, the harsh

A Jacobite Legacy

reprisals after Culloden, and the repression of the clan system, served to inflame anti-government feeling. After the rebellion of 1745, many of the clansmen had surrendered rusted and useless weapons in accordance with the demands of the Disarming Act, but had retained their serviceable arms for use during a future rising, so that Jacobite sentiment in Scotland was not to be easily extinguished.

As the years passed, and hopes for a Stuart succession gradually receded, true Jacobite sentiment gave way to romantic illusion, and the legend of Bonnie Prince Charlie was born. Fuelled by the publication of historical works such as Chambers' "History of the Rebellion, 1745-6", and "Jacobite Memoirs", detailing much of the work of Robert Forbes, a frustrated Jacobite who had painstakingly collected over a lifetime, first-hand accounts by people who had participated in the events of 1745-46, and of numerous other published accounts, the public imagination was captured by a new, romanticised version of the Prince's exploits. He was, after all, a heroic figure, who had very nearly succeeded in his ambitious project of restoring his father to the three thrones. His escape, after months spent in eluding capture by many hundreds of government militia as well as elements of the British navy, and assisted by no less a heroine than the beautiful Flora Macdonald, whilst in the guise of her maid, Betty Burke, surely belongs in the realms of romantic fiction. The fact that thousands of his followers lost their lives in support of his cause, whilst their families were left in abject poverty, seems to have been ignored by this latest generation of Jacobite sympathisers. So, too, were the unsavoury details of his later life, his fiery temper, his callous treatment of his closest adherents, his mental and physical cruelty to the women in his life, and his alcohol dependence, to which even in youth he had shown a great propensity. All this was forgotten in the new wave of Jacobite sentimentalism, whilst the great romantic novelist Sir Walter Scott

A Jacobite Legacy

added fuel to the flames with his exciting "Waverley", a story woven around the exploits of Macdonald of Tiendrish, and "Redgauntlet", another novel set in the period of the Forty-Five.

It was Scott, together with General Stewart of Garth, who engineered the visit of George IV to Edinburgh in 1822, with the rekindling of public interest in Highland dress and customs consequent on that visit. Scottish lairds as well as the English aristocracy duly kitted themselves out in tartan kilts and trews, with all the accompanying accoutrements, including pistols, powderhorns, and broadswords. Scottish romanticism was later further extended with the construction of Balmoral Castle by Queen Victoria, and her own love of Scotland and its romantic associations, and she herself became one of the first collectors of Jacobite memorabilia. McIan's beautifully illustrated book, "The Clans of the Scottish Highlands", with its accompanying historical text, was not only dedicated to the Queen, but was deliberately published in 1845, to coincide with the centenary of the outbreak of the Rebellion in 1745, and his portraits of the clansmen are to be found in every gift shop in Scotland to this day.

The Victorians soon emulated the monarch, and objects with Jacobite associations now became eminently collectable. Exhibitions of these memorabilia were held, where interested members of the public could indulge their romantic fantasies by gazing in awe at objects connected in some way or another, with the events of the previous century, and even in recent times, displays of memorabilia are held regularly, as in 1995, on the two hundred and fiftieth anniversary of the Rising, and again in the following year, to commemorate the two hundred and fiftieth anniversary of the Battle of Culloden. Such exhibitions have served over the years, to perpetuate sentimental and romantic elements of the Forty-Five. Schoolchildren rallying to the cry of "Highlanders and Redcoats!"

A Jacobite Legacy

in Scottish playgrounds during the '40's, were unwittingly re-enacting the events of two hundred years before, when the heroic Major Donald Macdonald of Tiendrish succeeded in capturing two companies of Royal Scots en route for Fort William, or when the luckless Captain Swetenham of Guise's regiment was captured by a band of Keppoch clansmen, so becoming the first prisoner to be taken during the campaign, both events taking place within days of the outbreak of the rising.

In Jacobite sentimentalism, it is only the happier elements of the period which survive. The perceived image is of a young and handsome Prince, who places himself at the head of his father's oppressed subjects, in support of a true and just cause, opposing the forces of evil as represented by Cumberland and his cruel, red-coated soldiers. The Prince is brave, yet merciful, his devoted clansmen imbued with zeal for his cause, and ready to lay down their lives to re-establish his father on the throne. Those professing an interest in the many items of Jacobite memorabilia to have survived until the present day, take a much broader and more balanced view of the Jacobite question. The Stuarts were dogged as much by bad luck as bad management. Their best schemes came to nought. James VIII comes across as a thoughtful and considerate individual, a caring father, yet a man totally devoid of charisma. Charles, landing on Eriskay as a young man of 25, was exactly the opposite, dynamic, forceful, but, above all, persuasive, and endowed with great personal charm. Charles had the impetuosity of youth, and therein lay the secret of his early success, but, as many others have done before and since, surrounded himself with sycophantic and ambitious admirers whose advice was at best unreliable, at worst, positively dangerous. It is not difficult to understand the reasons for the embitterment and alcoholism which dominated his later years. As with most people, he had good points as well as bad, the bold aims of his youth being gradually replaced

A Jacobite Legacy

by increasing frustration as his ambitions for further risings were thwarted one by one, whilst in desperation he sought solace more and more in the liquid refreshment on which he had come to depend.

It is interesting to reflect that had Charles Edward Stuart never landed in Scotland in 1745, what a void there would be, not only in our history and in our literature, but also in our poetry, as well as in our song.

* * * * *

A Jacobite Legacy

KEY

1. Abbotsford..(A)
2. Achnacarry House..(AH)
3. Baldwins...(B)
4. Beaufort Castle..(BC)
5. Blair Castle...(BrC)
6. Bonhams, 10/4/02...(B1)
7. Bonhams 10/6/02..(B2)
8. Bonhams 22/8/02..(B3)
9. British Museum...(BM)
10. Brodie Castle..(BeC)
11. Browseholme Hall...(BH)
12. Castello Theodoli, Italy..(CT)
13. Charlton Hall Galleries, USA....................................(CHG)
14. Chiddingstone Castle, Kent......................................(ChC)
15. Christie's Jacobite Sale, 12/6/96...............................(CJS)
16. Christie's Sale, 26/5/98..(CS1)
17. Christie's Sale, 16/11/99..(CS2)
18. Christie's Sale, Cheltenham, 6/02.............................(CS3)
19. Christie & Edmiston, 29/3/83...................................(C&E)
20. Clan Donald Museum..(CDdM)
21. Clan Donnachaidh Museum.....................................(CDhM)
22. Cortachie Castle..(CC)
23. Culloden Exhibition, 1996..(CE)
24. Derby Museum..(DyM)
25. Downham Hall..(DH)
26. Drambuie Collection, Edinburgh..............................(DC)
27. Drum Castle..(DmC)
28. Drumlanrig Castle..(DgC)
29. Duart Castle..(DtC)
30. Dumfries Museum...(DsM)
31. Dundee Museum & Art Gallery................................(DMAG)

A Jacobite Legacy

32. Dunvegan Castle...(DnC)
33. Eilean Donan Castle..(EDC)
34. Episcopal Palace, Montefiasconi, Italy.........................(EPM)
35. Exhibition of the Royal House of Stuart, 1889............(ERHS)
36. Fingask Castle Sale, 26/4/93.......................................(FCS)
37. Frascati Cathedral, Italy...(FC)
38. Frascati Palace, Italy..(FP)
39. Glamis Castle..(GC)
40. Glasgow International Exhibition, 1901......................(GIE)
41. Glasgow Museums...(GM)
42. Gorringes...(G)
43. Greenslade Sale, 1974..(GS)
44. Hall Fine Art..(HFA)
45. Highland & Jacobite Exhibition, Inverness, 1903..........(HJE)
46. Holyrood Palace..(HP)
47. Internet Auction..(IA)
48. Inventory, Bindon House, 1927.................................. (IBH)
49. Inverary Castle..(IC)
50. Inverness Museum..(IM)
51. Jacobite Anthology...(JA)
52. Jacobite & Stuart Exhibition, Edinburgh, 1952...............(JSE)
53. Kirkcudbright Museum..(KM)
54. Leith Hall...(LH)
55. Levens Hall..(LsH)
56. Lyon & Turnbull, 2002..(LT1)
57. Lyon & Turnbull 5/12/02...(LT2)
58. Macpherson Museum..(MnM)
59. Manchester Jacobites Exhibition, 1951.......................(MJE)
60. Marischal Museum..(MM)
61. Menzies Castle..(MC)
62. Montrose Museum..(MeM)
63. Moy Hall...(MH)
64. National Army Museum...(NAM)

A Jacobite Legacy

65. National Library of Scotland.......................................(NLS)
66. National Trust for Scotland..(NTS)
67. Naworth Castle...(NC)
68. Nicholas Shaw Antiques..(NSA)
69. North Carolina Dept of Cultural Resources...............(NCDR)
70. Northeast Auctions, USA..(NA)
71. Notarial Archives, Florence......................................(NAF)
72. Peter Wilson Auctioneers..(PW)
73. Phillips, New Bond Street...(PNB)
74. Phillips, Bayswater..(PB)
75. Phillips, Edinburgh, 2/7/99.......................................(PE1)
76. Phillips, Edinburgh, 26/8/00.....................................(PE2)
77. Precious Cargo Exhibition, Edinburgh, 1997...............(PCE)
78. Private Collection..(PC)
79. Railton Sale...(RS)
80. Rammerscales House..(RH)
81. Rowley Fine Art, 12/12/01..(RFA)
82. Royal Library, Windsor...(RLW)
83. Royal Museum of Scotland ....(RMS)
84. Royal State Archives, Rome.....................................(RSA)
85. Royal Stewart Society Exhibition, (CDhM1999)........(RSSE)
86. Scottish National Exhibition, 1911............................(SNE)
87. Scottish National Memorials, 1888...........................(SNM)
88. Scottish National Portrait Gallery.............................(SNPG)
89. Scottish Record Office..(SRO)
90. Scottish United Services Museum.............................(SUSM)
91. Shapes, Edinburgh, 1/7/70..(SE1)
92. Shapes, Edinburgh, 31/3/01......................................(SE2)
93. Society of Antiquaries of Newcastle upon Tyne.........(SANT)
94. Sotheby's, Gleneagles, 2000......................................(SG)
95. Sotheby's, New York...(SNY)
96. Sotheby's, West Sussex...(SWS)
97. The Blairs Museum, Deeside.....................................(TBM)

A Jacobite Legacy

98. Traquair House..(TH)
99. Tullie House Museum, Carlisle....................................(THM)
100. Wales & the Royal Stuarts Exhibition, Cardiff, 1934..(WRS)
101. West Highland Museum, Fort William......................(WHM)
102. Widdrington Collection..(WC)
103. Glendinings-Woolf Collection................................(G-WC)

It has been found convenient to reduce the source of each item to a particular set of initials, the full title of each source being given in the above key. Where objects have been itemised in more than one catalogue, each source is listed, the earliest occasion being given first. Items in private hands, but which have also been catalogued as being displayed at exhibitions, are listed only under the initials of the relevant exhibition.

A Jacobite Legacy

CATALOGUE

Admission ticket
 a) To private meetings of Jacobite societies.
A large number of Jacobite secret societies was in existence, where members met, possibly at some personal risk, to discuss the likely prospects of a Stuart restoration. A toast would be drunk at these meetings, to "The King over the Water". Around 140 of these societies or clubs were known. In Edinburgh, the Royal Oak Society was formed, in North Wales, the Cycle Club, one of the most famous of all such societies, founded by Sir Watkin Williams Wynn in 1710. South and West Wales were served by the Society of Sea Serjeants, which was in existence between 1726 and 1762. London boasted several Jacobite societies, particularly the Oak Society, which met at the Crown and Anchor Inn in the Strand, and which Prince Charles is reputed to have attended in 1750, and the Beaufort Society, named after Lord Beaufort, who was a prominent English Jacobite, whilst there were many equally active societies in the provinces.

 1) Around the edge of one is written: "Cha. Edw. Stuart, born Decr.20, 1720. Hen.Ben.Stuart, born Feb.23,1725." The birth dates are Old Style. (ERHS)
 2) Another, commemorating those who died in the cause. Around the edge is written: "James Fra. Edw. Stuart, born June 10, 1688; Mary Clementina Sobieska, died Jan.18, 1735, ag.33." (ERHS)
 3) Rose-shaped tickets, containing the names of 74 executed Jacobites. (BrC)
 4) Pair of rose admission tickets bearing the names of the Jacobite martyrs of 1746, framed. (WRS)
 5) Rose admission ticket bearing the names of the Royal Stuarts, and of the Jacobite martyrs of 1746. Mounted on blue paper, in a gilt frame. (WRS)

A Jacobite Legacy

6) Two rose admission tickets to meetings of the Cycle Club, printed with the names of the Jacobite martyrs of 1746.   (ChC)

7) Rose admission ticket bearing the names of the Jacobite martyrs of 1746, and of the Royal Stuarts. In contemporary gilt frame decorated with oak leaves and acorns.   (IA)

b) Admission ticket to the trials of the Earl of Kilmarnock, the Earl of Cromartie, and Lord Balmerino.   (DC)

c) Admission ticket to the Theatre Royal, Covent Garden, to commemorate the victory of the Duke of Cumberland at Culloden.   (BM)

d) Admission ticket (on card) to a seat in Lord Ancaster's box at the trial of Lord Lovat, framed.   (CE)

Aigrette
Made of dark-green feathers, formerly belonging to Prince Charles.   (ERHS)

Anvil
This is the anvil preserved at Moy Hall, reputed to have belonged to Donald Fraser, the blacksmith of Moy, who, with four others, was responsible for the incident known as the Rout of Moy, in which 1500 soldiers of Lord Loudoun's regiment were put to flight, and Macrimmon, the hereditary piper of the Lairds of Macleod, killed.   (MH, HJE)

Apron-string
Piece of, from the print dress worn by the Prince when dressed as Betty Burke, and attached to the front board of Volume III of *The Lyon in Mourning*.   (NLS)

Armchair
a) Which belonged to and was habitually used by Simon Fraser, Lord Lovat.   (HJE)

A Jacobite Legacy

b) Of oak, and used by the Prince whilst resting at an inn on the way to Culloden. The innkeeper borrowed the chair from nearby Darnaway Castle, and failed to return it. (SWS)

c) Pair, belonging to the Kerry Hunt, a Welsh Jacobite society. Each has a motto inscribed on a brass plaque. (WRS)

d) From Culloden House, and two other chairs, formerly in the bedroom occupied by Prince Charles. (GIE, SNE)

e) Said to have been occupied by the Prince while at Ellerton Grange, before entering Carlisle on his retreat from Derby. (THM)

f) Oak armchair sent by Cameron of Lochiel to the Prince at Glenfinnan. (WHM)

Armada chest
Of iron, its exterior painted with flowers and grotesque masks, and used by Bonnie Prince Charlie to store cess money whilst in Derby. (DyM)

Axe
Lochaber, found, together with two bombshells, in the cellar of a house in Montrose, and believed to date from the Jacobite occupation. (MeM)

* * * * *

Additional Notes: A

A Jacobite Legacy

A Jacobite Legacy

B

Badge

a) Gold-enamelled badge of the Lady Patroness of the Cycle Club, Lady Watkin Williams Wynn. Successive generations of the ladies of her family succeeded to this office. (WRS, ERHS) (See also Jewel)

b) Of cut steel, worn in memory of the Rising of 1745. (SNM)

c) Of the Order of St Andrew, which opens to reveal a miniature of Charles' wife, Princess Louise of Stolberg. Formerly belonging to Charles, bequeathed by him to his daughter, Charlotte, and by her to Cardinal Henry. It now forms part of the Scottish regalia. (SNE)

d) Of the Order of the Garter. Brought from England by James II and later belonging to Cardinal York. Forms part of the Scottish regalia. (SNE)

e) Gold, showing the Prince in campaign dress, after Sir Robert Strange. (SNE)

f) Silver, similar to above. (SNE)

g) Of white satin, bearing the names of the Jacobite martyrs of 1746, mounted in a round, gilt frame. (WRS)

h) Silver Jacobite badge, heart-shaped, engraved with a heart pierced by two arrows, dated 1648, and the words: " I live and dy in loyaltye". (IM)

i) Bronze cap badge adorned with a likeness of the Prince in highland dress. (ChC)

j) Similar cap badge. (BM)

Bagpipes

a) Belonging to Alister Macleod, (sic) piper, who died at Culloden. The pipes were found in his arms. (HJE)

A Jacobite Legacy

b) Belonging to John Mac-an Sgeulaich, and played by him in the battles of the Forty-Five as piper to the Atholl Brigade.
(BrC, SNE)

c) French bagpipes formerly belonging to Prince Charles, later inherited by Henry Benedict, and sold after his death. (RMS)

d) Set of bagpipes covered in Mackenzie tartan, said to have been carried at Culloden by a clansman from Baleshare, and known as the Great Pipes of Baleshare. (CE)

Ball

a) Lead, dug up by the plough at Culloden. (HJE)

b) Lead, three in number, found on Culloden field, along with a button. (GIE)

c) Lead musketball, excavated from Culloden battlefield, together with a handwritten note verifying its authenticity, and mounted in a wooden frame. (IA)

d) Two lead musketballs from the wreck of HMS Dartmouth, which sank in Tobermory Bay after returning from the bombardment of Armadale Castle, Skye, in 1690. (CDdM)

Ball Pouch

Used at the battle of Killiecrankie, still containing lead ball.
(HJE)

Banknotes   See under Lithograph.

Baptismal napkin

Of Bonnie Prince Charlie, made of damask linen. (SNM)

Bayonet

a) Of plug type, found on the battlefield of Killiecrankie.
(HJE)

b) Found on Culloden field. (HJE)

A Jacobite Legacy

Beaker   See also under Canteen.
Of horn, engraved with a thistle and Jacobite rose.   (DC)

Bed
During the marches of the Highland army, the Prince normally slept at the home of a local laird, not always a Jacobite. Some of these houses have long been demolished, but many have survived, and in a few of these, the bed in which the Prince traditionally slept, has been preserved.   (MH, DgC)

Bed-hangings
a) Taken from the bed on which the Prince slept, whilst staying at the house of Mrs Lowthian in Dumfries, 21 December, 1745.
(PC)
b) Taken from the bed at Culloden House on which the Prince slept on the morning of the battle of Culloden, and on the previous two nights.   (PE2)

Bible
a) family, belonging to John Ogilvy of Inshewen, Captain and Paymaster in the Forfarshire regiment.   (PC)
b) belonging to Lord George Murray.   (BrC)

Biretta   (See also Cap)
A square cap worn by Roman Catholic clerics, formerly belonging to Cardinal York.   (SNM)

Blanket
a) From Gortleg House, (sic) the home of Lovat's "doer", William Fraser.   (HJE)
b) A piece of the blanket under which the Prince lay when in Manchester, with an old label confirming this.   (WRS)
c) From Culloden House, on which the Prince is reputed to have slept on the night before the battle of Culloden.   (IM)

A Jacobite Legacy

Blunderbuss
 Flintlock blunderbuss by I Finch, with brass barrel engraved "Taken at the battle of Culloden 16th April 1746 by Capt John Goodenough with 18 balls in it." (WKNF)

Bodkin
 Belonging to Flora Macdonald, and used by her as a hairpin. (ERHS, FCS)

Bombshell
 a) Pair, found in the cellar of a house in Montrose, together with a Lochaber axe, and believed to date from the Jacobite occupation. (MeM)
 b) Recovered from the postmaster's house in Montrose after the shelling of the town by HM sloop Hazard in 1745. (MeM)

Bonnet
 a) Belonging to Bonnie Prince Charlie, and left by him at Moy Hall on Monday 17 February, 1746. (MH, HJE)
 b) Reputed to be the same bonnet left by the Prince at Moy Hall! (WHM)
 c) Given by the Prince to Stewart Threipland, and by the latter to Laurence Oliphant of Gask. (SNM, GIE)
 d) Blue bonnet with white cockade, left at Carlisle on the retreat of the highland army. (THM)
 e) Jacobite bonnet, found buried in a peat bog 3 feet underground. (IM)
 f) Bonnet belonging to a French officer, and left by him at the Half Moon Inn, Brampton, together with a dress sword. (PC)

Books
 a) Two books covered with the skin of a greyhound, presented to the Threipland family by Bonnie Prince Charlie. (FCS)

A Jacobite Legacy

b) Book with embroidered velvet cover formerly belonging to Prince James. (ERHS)

c) Books from the library of Henry, Cardinal York, adorned with his coat of arms. (NLS)

d) Ecclesiastical history formerly belonging to Prince Charles, adorned with his coat of arms. (NLS)

e) Book read by Lord Balmerino during his confinement in the Tower, entitled: "De Criminibus", by Mattheus. It contains annotations and passages underlined, intended to help him in his defence, as well as his signature. (DC)

f) Order book of the highland army, in vellum binding, covering the period of the march into England until its return to Stirling. (SNE)

g) Memorandum book of gold and agate, with a gold pencil. Given by Charlotte, Duchess of Albany, in May 1788, to Henrietta-Antonia, Countess of Powis. It bears the arms of the Wynne and Herbert (Powis) families. (WRS)

h) Minute-books of the Cycle Club, two, from Nerquis Hall, Mold, Flintshire. They cover the period April, 1770, to February, 1864. (WRS)

i) Collection of books from the library of Lord George Murray's home in Holland, and used by him in exile. (BrC)

j) Missal belonging to Henry Benedict, bound in red velvet, the letter "H" embroidered on the front board in blue and gold. (FP)

k) Book of Hours belonging to Henry Benedict, bound in grey velvet with his monogram. Formerly belonged to Catherine de Medici. (FP)

l) Book of Common Prayer dated 1687, formerly belonging to James VII. (GIE)

m) Collection of Scottish Country Dances, written for the Duke of Perth in 1737, in contemporary binding. (GIE)

n) Letter-book belonging to Macdonnell of Glengarry. (GIE)

A Jacobite Legacy

o) The Life of Vincent de Paul, Rome, 1729, in a red morocco binding adorned with the arms of Clementina Sobieska. (ChC)

p) Book from the library of Henry IX, adorned with his arms, surmounted by a cardinal's hat. (ChC)

q) Book of Hours edited by Henry, Cardinal York, 1756, the front board decorated with a crown and lion rampant. (ChC)

r) Regole del Guico de Passi, Vienna, 1769, with Italian binding bearing the Royal Arms of Charles III. (ChC)

s) Book of Hours from the library of Cardinal Henry, formerly belonging to the Sobieski family, 14th century. (RLW)

Book-cover

a) Of gilt red morocco, with the Royal Arms and cardinal's hat of Henry Benedict. (WRS)

c) Of gilt red morocco, with the Royal Arms and cardinal's hat of Henry Benedict. (RMS)

Bookplate

Belonging to Cardinal York. Oval-shaped, and constructed of copper, it bears the Royal Arms of Great Britain and Ireland, surmounted by a cardinal's hat. (SNE)

Bowl

a) China, belonging to Flora Macdonald. (HJE, SNE)

b) With saucer, used by George Seton, fifth Earl of Winton, during his confinement in the Tower in 1716. (SNM)

c) Delftware, with a portrait of Charles. (BM)

d) Delftware, with a male portrait head inside, and "Confusion to the Pretender 1746". (BM)

Box

a) Of silver, and small dimensions, formerly belonging to Flora Macdonald. (HP)

A Jacobite Legacy

b) Gold-mounted, and of French manufacture, with a miniature of the Prince set into the outside of the lid. (HP)

c) With tartan decoration, having a double lid with a secret portrait of the Prince, the inside in the form of a reliquary. Said to have belonged to Clementina Walkinshaw, the Prince's mistress. (KM, SNM)

d) Beaded, and containing a lock of Prince Charles Edward's hair. (TH)

e) Tortoiseshell box given by Bonnie Prince Charlie to Patrick Grant, one of the Seven Men of Glenmoriston. (HP)

f) Silver box with concealed portrait of the Prince. (RMS)

g) Gold box with secret dispatches, given by Prince Charles to Sir Robert Strange. (ERHS)

h) Silver box inscribed with text, presented by James II to Ludovic Innes, thence to Lord Lovat. (HJE)

i) Circular box containing the marriage medal of James and Clementina, the box lid with another likeness of the latter on the outside. The Prince carried this object with him, and is said to have given it, along with a small travelling canteen, to Dr Murdoch Macleod. (HJE)

j) Belonging to the Mackintoshes, which was buried along with valuables and papers during 1715 and 1745 rebellions. (HJE)

k) Box in the form of a cameo depicting a scene of a stag pursued by dogs, having a gold lid engraved with the scene of a highlander holding a branch, and containing silver and pebble shirt studs, which formerly belonged to Prince Charles. (SNM)

l) With miniature of Clementina set inside the lid. (CDM, RSSE)

m) Circular, formerly belonging to James II, and given by him to the Jacobite, Lord John Caryll. (HP)

n) Dice, with concealed portrait of the Prince. (IM)

o) Circular horn box reliquary, containing the blood, hair, and Garter ribbon of King James II. (ChC)

A Jacobite Legacy

p) Pinchbeck box, the lid bearing a portrait of the Prince in highland dress, and containing a small print of the Strange engraving of Charles. (WC)

q) Box with a concealed portrait of the Prince wearing highland dress. (WC)

r) Box for hairpins, formerly belonging to Flora Macdonald. (WC)

s) Ivory box, its lid carved in relief with a scene depicting the Prince's birth. (WC, WHM)

t) Boxes containing lead shot from HMS Dartmouth. (RMS)

Bracelet

a) Pair, made from Prince Charles' curb spur chains. (HJE)

b) A gift of Prince Charles, together with a necklace and cross, and a steelwork medallion. (ERHS)

c) Gold engraved bracelet, with lid concealing his miniature, and inscribed: "Prince Charles Edward, taken while at Breakfast at Blair Atholl, 1st September 1745". (BrC, SNE)

Breastplate

Belonging to Viscount Graham of Claverhouse. (SNE)

Breviary

Belonging to Bishop Hugh Macdonald of Morar, who blessed the Prince's standard at Glenfinnan in 1745. (CDdM)

Bridle

a) Of leather, iron, and brass, belonging to William Boyd, 4th Earl of Kilmarnock, executed for treason 18 August 1746. (CE)

b) From the battlefield of Sheriffmuir, 1715. (SNM, HJE)

A Jacobite Legacy

Brocade, silk
Fragment of, from Lady Clanranald's wedding dress. (CJS)
Brogues
Worn by the Prince whilst disguised as "Betty Burke". (PC)

Brooch
a) Bronze plaid brooch found at Culloden Moor. (ERHS)
b) Silver brooch worn by the Prince when in hiding. (ERHS, SNE)
c) Diamond key-shaped brooch said to have been presented to Flora Macdonald by the Prince. (ERHS, LT2, IA)
d) Diamond brooch containing a lock of his hair, given by the Prince to John Kinloch of Kibrie and Logie, at Versailles, in 1750. (ERHS, GIE)
e) Pearl brooch containing locks of Flora's and Charles' hair. (SNM, ERHS, HJE)
f) Silver brooch inscribed at the rear with the Prince's initials, believed to have been worn by him when in the guise of Betty Burke, and given by him at Portree to Flora Macdonald. (HJE)
g) Paste brooch of crescent shape, formerly belonging to Flora. (SNM, HJE, ERHS)
h) Pendant brooch, worked in the hair of her two dead sons, by Flora Macdonald. (HJE)
i) Containing a lock of the Prince's hair, clipped by Flora Macdonald, and given by her to Mrs Macdonald of Kingsburgh. (HJE)
j) Celtic brass brooch, worn by Alexander Finlay, weaver, of Elgin, who fought at Culloden. (HJE)
k) Celtic brass brooch worn by William Chaumers of Caputh, Dunkeld, who fought at Culloden. (HJE)
l) Silver heart brooch, made from an English coin picked up on Culloden field by Duncan Ruagh Macrimmon of Glenelg, who fought there that day. (HJE)

A Jacobite Legacy

m) Gold witch (luckenbooth) brooch belonging to Alexander Macdonald of Kingsburgh. (HJE)

n) Gold enamelled and jewelled brooch, with a lock of Prince Charles' hair. (ERHS)

o) Enamel and paste brooch depicting Aphrodite in a shell chariot drawn by two sea horses, containing a lock of Charles' hair, inscribed "A lock of Prince Charles Edward's hair cut 1763". (PC)

p) Plaid brooch belonging to Charles Stewart of Ardshiel. (CDM, RSSE)

q) Brooch containing a lock of the Prince's hair. (SNE)

r) Brooch in the form of two entwined hearts and a coronet, in coloured enamels. Formerly belonged to Flora Macdonald. (WRS)

s) Brooch formed from a miniature of the Prince. (WRS)

t) Brooch consisting of a button cut from Charles' coat. (WRS)

u) Jacobite rose brooch. (IM)

v) Crystal brooch and a pair of crystal earrings, presented by the Prince to John Farquarson of Allargue and his wife in 1750. (IM)

w) Gold brooch in the form of the Scottish crown, composed of garnets and seed pearls. The reverse is inscribed: "Do Come". (PC)

x) Jacobite rose brooch consisting of a crown surmounting a five-petalled rose. (IM)

y) Highland brooch containing a lock of Prince Charles' hair. (GIE)

z) Prince Charles Edward's plaid brooch. (GIE)

Buckle
 a) Belt
  1) Of silver and parcel gilt, presented by Bonnie Prince

A Jacobite Legacy

Charlie to the Laird of Mackinnon, and inscribed at the rear: "Carolus Princeps Deo Patriae Tibi". (PC)
    2) Which belonged to Flora Macdonald. (HJE)
    3) Belonging to Prince Charles Edward. (MnM)
  b) Plaid
    Of silver decorated with flowers, presented to Bonnie Prince Charlie by Finlay Macrae. Inscribed: "Tearlach Stuart Righ non Gael 1745". (IM)
  c) Shoe
    1) Pair, of silver and paste, formerly belonging to Bonnie Prince Charlie. (WHM)
    2) Pair, formerly belonging to Colonel Nairn. (WHM)
    3) Pair, worn by Bonnie Prince Charlie. (WHM)
    4) Pair, belonging to Flora Macdonald. (WHM)
    5) Pair, of paste and silver, worn at a reception for the Prince at Dumfries in 1745, together with a cross. (WHM)
    6) Pair, of brass, found at Culloden. (CJS)
    7) Pair, lent to Charles for the ball at Lude House, 2 September 1745. (CDhM)
    8) Belonging to Simon Fraser, Lord Lovat, along with garter and belt buckles. (SNE)
    9) Of silver and paste, presented by Charles to a Macdonald in exchange for his own. (WHM)
    10) Of silver and paste, presented by the Prince to John Roy Stewart. (CDdM)
    11) Pair, found on Culloden battlefield. (EDC)
  d) Knee
    1) Of silver, inscribed "C.S", presented to Mrs Murray of Broughton by the Prince. (ERHS)
    2) Belonging to an officer in the highland army, found at Culloden. (MH, HJE)
  e) Mourning
    In memory of John, Marquis of Tullibardine, killed

A Jacobite Legacy

Malplaquet 1709, and sent by his brother William, the then Marquis, as a token to Robertson of Faskally in 1715.   (BrC)

Bulletmould
Made of stone, used by the highland army, and left by them at Lochar Moss, where it was found.   (HJE, CE, GIE)

Burgess ticket
Of Royal Burgh of Inverness, in favour of Lady Anne Mackintosh of Macintosh, admitting her as "Burgess freewoman and Guild-sister".   (HJE)

Bust
a) Of Charles Edward Stuart, one of several known to have been made in plaster, from the original bronze by Jean Baptiste Lemoyne. The original is now lost.   (DC)
b) Of Charles Edward Stuart, in coloured wax. 4.75" high.   (PC)
c) Of Charles Edward Stuart, in bronze, after Lemoyne.   (SNPG)
d) Of Henry Benedict, Cardinal York, in marble. (FP, CT)
e) Of William, Duke of Cumberland, in Chelsea porcelain.   (BM)

Button
a) Belonging to Prince Charles.   (MH)
b) Eight tunic buttons found at Culloden.   (GS)
c) Four cairngorm buttons from Charles' kilt and vest.   (ERHS)
d) Four silver-wire buttons taken from the Prince's clothes at Edinburgh.   (SNM, ERHS)
e) Silver button from the Prince's kilt coat, given by him to his servant, Peter Macdonald, along with others.   (HJE)

A Jacobite Legacy

f) Turned up by the plough at Culloden. (HJE)

g) Eleven silver buttons, engraved with Jacobite roses. (MM)

h) Of the Cycle Club, in Sheffield plate, attached to a Cycle list. This has been pasted on wood, and varnished. (WRS)

i) Mounted as a brooch, and said to have been cut from Charles' coat. (WRS)

j) Of the Cycle Club. 19th century, made of Sheffield plate. (WRS)

k) Set of Cycle Club buttons, 19th century, of Sheffield plate, worn by Col. C J Trevor-Roper of Plas Teg, Flintshire. (WRS)

l) Twelve, belonging to Cardinal Henry Benedict, each in the form of an orb of rock crystal bound with longitudinal and horizontal silver bands, and surmounted by a cross. Commissioned by Henry in his role as Henry IX. See also Caddinet. (PC)

m) Dug up at Culloden field, together with three lead balls. (GIE)

n) Silver button of the Cycle Club, adorned with a wreath of oak leaves, circa 1780. (ChC)

o) Silver button engraved with a head and shoulders portrait of the Duke of Cumberland. (WHM)

* * * * *

Additional Notes: B

A Jacobite Legacy

A Jacobite Legacy

C

Cabinet
Of walnut, and small dimensions, containing a portrait of the Prince after Hussey, and used at meetings of the Cycle Club.
(PC)

Caddinet
A ceremonial place setting used for state banquets, belonging to Henry Benedict. It is silver gilt, and consists of a tray mounted on four feet, incorporating a double-lidded spice box, and having recesses for two pairs of gold-plated knives, forks, and tablespoons. The tray carries Henry's coat of arms as Henry IX, and the whole was fabricated in Rome by Luigi Valadier.   (HP)

Cameo
a) Jewelled, of the Prince, set in onyx, with filigree lid. (PC)
b) Unmounted, depicting Charles Edward Stuart. (RMS)

Camp kettle
Of copper, with folding handle, said to have been left at Drumlanrig Castle after the retreat of the highland army.   (DgC)

Candlestick
a) Glass, used by King James III, and presented to the Threipland family in 1854.   (FCS)
b) Pair, of wood mounted with brass, formerly belonging to Bonnie Prince Charlie, and taken at Culloden. (GIE ,HJE, CJS)
c) Pair, of amber and silver, formerly belonging to James II.
(WHM)
d) From Holyrood Palace, and used by Bonnie Prince Charlie.   (HJE)

A Jacobite Legacy

e) Used by the Prince on the night he slept at Ruskie, in the inn occupied by Daniel Fisher. (SNM)

Cannon

a) Iron. Used by the highland army in the siege of Fort William, it was constructed of iron covered with leather. (WHM)

b) Iron. On wooden carriage with wheels, used by the highland army on its march south. (SNM, GIE)

c) Iron. Taken from the wreck of La Fine. (MeM)

d) Two iron six-pounders, used in the defence of Carlisle against the highland army in 1745. (CC)

Cannonball

Various cannonball are known, unearthed at the scene of Jacobite battlefields. One has been fitted with a silver collar, inscribed "Ogilvy Culloden, 16 April 1746". Several cannonballs found at Culloden were exhibited in Inverness in 1903, during the Highland and Jacobite Exhibition there, and another, fired by Cumberland's army at the walls of Carlisle Castle, is still preserved in the castle. Two cannonballs have been unearthed at Fort Augustus, relics of its siege in 1746, whilst three more from HMS Dartmouth have been preserved, two of which, now in Clan Donald Museum, Skye, were fired at Armadale Castle in 1690.

(MM, PC's, HJE, CC, RMS, CDdM)

Canteen, travelling

a) This comprises a silver-gilt engraved beaker, with folding knife, fork, and spoon, together with a double-lidded spice box, all contained in a wooden, shagreen-covered box, said to have been carved by Prince Charles himself. (HJE, BeC)

b) Silver-gilt travelling canteen comprising 31 items, including two-piece knives, forks, and spoons, a nutmeg grater, corkscrew, and two beakers. The container is chased in rococo style, and

A Jacobite Legacy

engraved with Prince of Wales' feathers. It was recovered from the Prince's baggage after Culloden. (RMS)

Cap
Lace, forming part of the vestments of Cardinal Henry. (WRS)

Card case
Belonging to Princess Louise of Stolberg. (ERHS)

Casket
a) Of carved ivory, the sides showing biblical scenes, formerly belonging to Henry Benedict, its lockplate decorated with the arms of Henry IX. (PC)
b) Rectangular horn casket, left by the Prince at Fassifern House, home of John Cameron, Lochiel's brother. (CDdM)

Cast
Plaster, of the head of Simon Fraser, Lord Lovat, taken after his execution in 1747. (HJE)
(See also Death mask)

Catalogue
In manuscript, of Lord George Murray's library at Tullibardine Castle. (WRS)

Chair
a) Two, from Lord President Forbes' bedroom at Culloden House, occupied by Charles in April 1746, together with an armchair from the same source. (GIE)
b) Chair from Culloden House. (SNE)
c) Set of chairs covered in leather, decorated with the coat of arms of Henry, Cardinal York. (FP)
d) From Old Gask, on which the Prince sat during his visit there on September 11, 1745. (PC)

A Jacobite Legacy

Chanter-pipe
Made of ebony, and is all that remains of a set left in a house at the Haugh, Inverness, during the flight from Culloden. (HJE)

Chatelaine
Of silver gilt, belonging to Flora Macdonald. (HJE, SNE)

Christening robe
Of Prince Charles Edward. (PC)

Clasp
a) With a tree, worked in hair by Flora Macdonald. (SNM, ERHS, HJE)
b) For a Sea Serjeant's cloak, consisting of a pair of pinchbeck dolphins. (WRS)

Cloak
Of tartan, formerly belonging to Prince Charles. (SNM, ERHS, GIE)

Clothes
Tartan suit of, belonging to the English Jacobite, Sir John Hynde Cotton. (RMS)

Coat
a) Tartan coat belonging to Prince Charles Edward Stuart. (ERHS, GIE)
b) Tartan coat worn by one of the Prince's attendants at Culloden. (HJE)
c) Buff, belonging to Graham of Claverhouse, Viscount Dundee. (SNE)
d) Tartan coat and kilt belonging to Donald Stewart of Dunkeld, who was "out" in the Forty-Five. (SNE)

A Jacobite Legacy

Coat-of-arms
Of the Royal House of Stuart, constructed from quilled paper, gilded, and bearing the motto "Nemo Me Impune Lacesset". Circa 1700. (ChC)

Cockade, White
Some examples of the white cockade have survived, for example, those worn by Lord George Murray, Robert Strange, and Prince Charles Edward Stuart. The six-petalled white rose was adopted by the Jacobites as their symbol from the earliest times, and contrasted starkly with the black rose worn by the Hanoverians. They were made normally of white silk ribbon, sometimes of linen or paper, and were worn in the bonnet.
(SNM, RMS, BrC, TM, PC)

Coffee mill
Made of wood, and used by the Prince when in hiding.
(SNM, ERHS, GIE)

Coggie
Used by Charles when in hiding in South Uist, and formerly in the possession of descendants of Flora Macdonald. (ChC)

Coins
a) Crown piece of Charles II, which was hollow, and served to conceal messages between the clan chiefs during the '45. (HJE)
b) Halfpenny of George II, inscribed "Capt. Andw. Wood of the Rebel Army Gave me this Halfy July 28 1745 while Confind Wm Stapely. (JA)

Coin box
Belonging to King James VIII. (PC)

A Jacobite Legacy

Collar
Lace collar and ruffles said to have been given by Prince Charles in lieu of wages, together with a handkerchief purported to be stained with the tears of his daughter Charlotte. (WHM)

Colours, Regimental
Of Barrel's Regiment. (RMS)

Combs
Double-sided tortoiseshell, contained in a commemorative case, together with other relics of Bonnie Prince Charlie, including locks of his hair and a miniature. (RS)

Compass
a) Of ivory, used by Charles when in hiding. Given to the 4th Duke of Atholl by Lady Clerk in 1819. (BrC)
b) Jacobite compass, the letters N, S, E, W, being substituted by those of F, I, A and T, ie. "Fiat" (ChC)

Copper plate
a) For printing paper money. Fabricated by Prince Charles' artist and engraver, Sir Robert Strange, at Inverness. Recovered at the west end of Loch Laggan about 1835.
(SNM, ERHS, GIE, WHM)
b) For the production of souvenir copies of Hogarth's drawing of Simon, Lord Lovat, framed within a calendar for the year 1747. These were intended to be set in watch cases. The plate was subsequently used as a Fellowship Porter's badge for the City of London in 1777, and is so engraved on the reverse. (G-WC)
c) Celebrating the Duke of Cumberland's victory at the Battle of Lauffeld in 1747, and engraved with his likeness, and the words: "May Cumberland and his Flanders Band, Humble Scot and Gallic Land, 1747. (G-WC)

A Jacobite Legacy

Corkscrew See under Canteen

Costume
Of silk brocade, belonging to Bonnie Prince Charlie. (ERHS)

Cowhorn
Of large dimensions, having an iron suspension handle, the lid missing, and the body inscribed: "R B". Found on the battlefield of Prestonpans, and believed to have been used to carry lead ball. (PC)

Creepy
Or stool, used by Charles Edward.   (SNE)

Crucifix
Of bronze, belonging to Prince Charles.   (SNM, GIE)

Cuff, lace
In silver-mounted leather folder, the cuff embroidered; "God Save King James VIII".   (FCS, PC)

Cufflinks See sleevelinks

Cups and saucers
a) Pink china, adorned with gold wavy stripes, with a rose in the centre of the bowl. Formerly belonging to Flora Macdonald. (HJE, WHM)
b) Green and white china, out of which Prince Charles drank tea at Kingsburgh House.   (HJE)
c) Liverpool pottery cup, decorated with a portrait of Charles within a cartouche, and bearing the words: "Ab Obice Major".   (ChC)
d) Saltglaze cup, dated 1753, and initialled "IF", depicting highlanders, Jacobite roses and thistles.   (HFA)

A Jacobite Legacy

e) Jackfield pottery cups, three, decorated in gold on black glaze, depicting Charles in campaign dress, together with a thistle.
(BH)

Cushion

a) Silk, embroidered in Royal Stuart tartan with the Royal Cypher. (HJE)

b) Silk, bearing the names of the executed Jacobites, with the words: "Mart. for K. and Con. 1746". (SNM)

c) Silk, covered in Royal Stuart tartan, with the initials: "PC", worked in gold within a cartouche, surmounted by a crown and Prince of Wales' feathers, together with thistles and the date: "1745". (RFA)

Cutlery

a) Knife and fork with bone handles, traditionally held to have been used by Prince Charles during his stay in Dumfries. Formerly in the possession of the Gordons of Crogo, near Balmaclellan. (DsM)

b) Knife and fork originally belonging to James III. The handles are agate, of tapering octagonal form. (HP)

c) Two Edinburgh silver spoons, buried by Alexander Cameron of Glenevis in Somerled's cave in Glenevis in 1745, when he hid there with his family. (WHM)

d) 3 silver teaspoons, one engraved "JR", beneath a coronet, dated 1715, the others with the same cypher, and "Moyses Brittanicus". (FCS)

e) Gilt teaspoon formerly belonging to Prince Henry Benedict, and bequeathed by him, along with a majolica dish, to George III. (HP)

f) Horn spoon used by Bonnie Prince Charlie.
(SNM, ERHS)

g) Tablespoon formerly owned by Flora Macdonald.
(SNM, ERHS)

A Jacobite Legacy

h) Four silver tablespoons formerly owned by Flora Macdonald. Marked "AMD FMD" (ERHS, HJE)

i) Silver desert spoon in a case, the spoon crudely inscribed: "This was the Pretender's." (ERHS)

j) Six silver teaspoons, hallmarked for 1745, engraved "C.R." (ERHS)

k) Silver spoon, knife and fork, in a leather case, the spoon marked: "Ex. Dono C.P.R. July 3d 1746". This was the set given by the Prince to Murdoch Macleod on that date, saying "Keep that till I see you". (HJE, RMS, GIE)

l) Black shagreen case containing a large knife, three smaller knives, a fork, and a larding pin, all with gilt and chased handles. Said to have belonged to Bonnie Prince Charlie. (ERHS)

m) Knife and fork with silver handles, belonging to Alexander Robertson of Struan, the Jacobite poet. (SNM)

n) Silver-mounted knife and fork which belonged to Flora Macdonald. (SNM)

o) 3 silver forks used at the banquet given for the Prince by Mrs Robertson of Lude, 1745. (CDhM)

p) Silver desert spoon, in a silver-gilt casket, used by Prince Charles Edward. (GIE)

Cymbals

Pair, constructed of iron, said to have been used as targes by Macdonalds at Culloden, and picked up from the field. (SNE)

* * * * *

A Jacobite Legacy

Additional Notes: C

A Jacobite Legacy

D

Death mask
    a) Plaster cast, said to have been taken after death from Bonnie Prince Charlie by Bernadine Lucheese. (CJS)
    b) Wax death mask of James II. (ERHS)
    c) Wax death mask of James Radcliffe, Earl of Derwentwater, executed on Tower Hill in 1716. (SANT)
    d) Bronze cast of the death mask of King Charles III. (Bonnie Prince Charlie) (IM)

Decanter
    a) Of the Shrewsbury Hunt, 1769-99, one of the "True Blue" hunts, a known Jacobite Society. (WRS)
    b) Used by the Cycle Club, which met at the house of Daniel Porter in Wrexham. (WRS)

Despatch box
    a) Used by the Prince. (PC)
    b) Of Field Marshall James Keith, circa 1715. (MM)

Devotion book
    Belonging to Flora Macdonald. (WHM)

Dice box
    Containing dice, and with a portrait of Bonnie Prince Charlie on the inner lid. (IM)

Die, steel
    a) For Oak Society medal, fabricated by Thomas Pingo. The society met regularly at the Crown and Anchor Inn in the Strand. The medal has a portrait of Prince Charles on the obverse, and a

A Jacobite Legacy

withered oak on the reverse, from which a new shoot is emerging. The legend reads: "Revirescit" - "It grows green again". (ERHS)

b) Belonging to Cardinal York, with a Latin inscription, and bearing the royal arms of Great Britain and Ireland, surmounted by a cardinal's hat. (SNE)

Dirks

Together with other weaponry of the period, these are designated Jacobite, either from their association with Jacobite battlefields, or known Jacobites. Two such are in the West Highland Museum, the first carried by Duncan Cameron of Dochnassie at Prestonpans, whilst the second was presented by the Prince to Donald Cameron of Glenpean. Bonnie Prince Charlie's own dirk is amongst those to have survived. A brass-mounted dirk made in Innerwick, Glenlyon, by a smith named Macfarlane, is said to have been carried throughout the Forty-Five by John Macnaughton, and a similar one was found in the roof of King's Stables, near Culloden. Another dirk, the blade, as with many other dirks, made from an old backsword, is said to have belonged to Duncan MacGregor of Roro, who served as an officer in the Atholl Brigade in 1745. A dirk of crude workmanship, whose blade is taken from an old backsword, is reputed to have been constructed by a Loch Tayside blacksmith, carried by himself during the 1715 Rising, and by his son during the '45, and there are many other instances of such dirks, whose past history has been passed down through succeeding generations.

Dish

a) Of silver, belonging to Princess Louise of Stolberg. (HJE)

b) Of majolica ware, adorned with the arms of Henry Benedict, and bequeathed by him, together with a gilt teaspoon, to George III. (HP)

c) Of delftware, bearing an equestrian portrait of the Duke of Cumberland. (BM)

A Jacobite Legacy

d) Silver, with lid, presented to Clementina on the birth of Charles. Made by Angelo Spinazzi, Rome, circa 1720. See also Écuelle. (SG)
e) Delftware, belonging to Flora Macdonald. (GIE)

Documents

A large number of documents related to the Jacobite era has survived. Many are concerned with the rising of 1745, and vary from simple receipts for goods and supplies ordered by the highland army, to regimental orders, and commissions granted to individual officers. A great deal of personal correspondence has also survived, amongst them letters from Lord George Murray, Macpherson of Cluny, Cameron of Lochiel, and Prince Charles himself. In the Stuart Papers, the property of Her Majesty the Queen, much of the correspondence between Charles and his father has been preserved, whilst on the Hanoverian side, many of the letters of Duncan Forbes, Lord President of the Court of Session, who played such a key role in quelling the rising, are also still in existence. Other documentation in the form of Acts of Parliament relating to Disarming, Heritable Jurisdictions, and Attainder, proclamations, marriage and baptismal certificates, maps and battle plans, warrants, safe conducts, ship's log, newspapers, pamphlets, gaol registers, and dying declarations, has also survived. The ship's log referred to, is that of Le du Teillay, the frigate belonging to Antoine Walsh, in which the Prince sailed to Scotland. It gives full details of the engagement fought between her escort vessel, L'Élisabeth, and HMS Lyon. In addition, many individual accounts of events, particularly in relation to the Forty-Five, have been written by participants on both sides of the conflict, and have fortunately been preserved for posterity. These include narratives by Prince Charles Edward, Lord George Murray, John William O'Sullivan, Felix O'Neill, John Roy Stuart, the Chevalier de Johnstone, Donald Cameron of Lochiel, James Maxwell of Kirkconnell, Lord Elcho,

A Jacobite Legacy

Neil McKeachan, John Murray of Broughton, John Home, Robert Strange, Donald Macleod, James Ray, and numerous others, less well known but of equal fascination. (Sources include, amongst others, the National Library of Scotland, National Museums of Scotland, and the Scottish Record Office.)

Dog-collar
Of silver, presented by Bonnie Prince Charlie to the Threipland family, and engraved "C.Stewartus Princeps. Juventutis", and, "Collar of an Italian Greyhound presented by Prince Charles Edward Stuart to Sir Stuart Threipland or Lady Threipland in the year 1750". (SNM, ERHS, FCS)

Domino box
Belonging to the Duke of Cumberland, and engraved with his monogram. Left by him at Culloden House. (MH, HJE)

Draughts piece
a) Consisting of a wooden copy of a medal commemorating the English victory at the Battle of La Hogue, 1692. (B)
b) Similar, commemorating the bombardment of the French coast by the English in 1694. (B)

Drawing
a) Of Prince Charles. (HP)
b) Of a head, said to have been executed by Prince Charles when a boy. (ERHS, GIE)

Dress
a) Piece of silk dress formerly belonging to Flora Macdonald. (SNM, ERHS)
b) Of reddish-brown satin brocaded with a pattern of rose sprays. Said to have been worn by Lady Margaret Ogilvie, daughter

A Jacobite Legacy

of Sir William Johnstone of Westerhall, when she opened the ball given at Holyrood Palace by the Prince. (JSE)

c) Piece of, worn by Bonnie Prince Charlie when dressed as Betty Burke, and attached by Robert Forbes to the front board of Vol III of The Lyon in Mourning. (NLS)

Drinking-cup

a) Of silver, used by Prince Charles in 1745. Engraved with the royal arms of Scotland, and "In defence", and "Nemo me impune lacesset", with the initials "C.P.R." (RMS, ERHS, GIE)

b) Of silver, said to have been used by the Prince, and inscribed: "A.McD.to M.N. 1763". This was a gift from Allan Macdonald, husband of Flora. (SNM, ERHS)

c) Belonging to Charles. (SNE)

* * * * *

Additional Notes: D

A Jacobite Legacy

A Jacobite Legacy

E

Earrings
a) Of Scottish stones, worn by Flora Macdonald.
(SNM, ERHS)
b) Pair of agate earrings given by Flora Macdonald to Lady Wynn, widow of Sir Watkin Williams Wynn.   (WRS)
c) Pair of crystal earrings presented by the Prince to John Farquarson of Allargue and his wife, Anne, in 1750, along with a crystal brooch.   (IM)

Écuelle   See under Dish

Engravings
Like miniatures and medals, as well as portraiture, engravings were in effect the publicity or propaganda of their day, so that it is hardly surprising that the subject of many of the engravings of the Jacobite period is frequently Prince Charles Edward Stuart. Popular paintings were reproduced on copper plates by the engraver, and the printed images were then distributed or sold to those interested in acquiring them. Engravings were easy to manufacture, and could be produced cheaply in large numbers. Street engravings of the Prince were offered for sale at public places, racecourses and theatres, as well as in the towns occupied by the highland army during its march south into England, the aim being, to attract as much publicity as possible, and to encourage the local populace to join their ranks. The French engraver, Nicolas Edelinck, made engravings of both of the young princes, after portraits by Antonio David, and that of Prince Charles was later adapted by Robert Strange and sold during the Forty-Five. Sir Robert produced the only engraving of the Prince thought to have been made during the rebellion. Occasionally the engraving will be coloured, as in one

A Jacobite Legacy

example by Richard Cooper, but most are in monochrome. The French engravers J. Daullé, Michel Aubert, and N.J.B. de Poilly also printed engravings of the Prince. Other popular subjects of the engraver's art were James III, by both Edelinck and Largillière, his consort, Clementina, and Simon Fraser, the Jacobite Lord Lovat, engraved by Hogarth. The funerals of James and of Clementina were both commemorated in engravings of the period, and "The Execution of the Rebel Lords on Tower Hill" was the title of yet another. A further type of engraving popular during the eighteenth century was the satirical engraving, produced by Jacobites as well as anti-Jacobites. Examples of the former were "The Agreable Contrast", which compared the handsome Prince with the obese figure of the Duke of Cumberland, and "A Race from Preston Pans to Berwick", a satire on the flight of Sir John Cope, whilst on the Hanoverian side, there was a whole host of satirical engravings, "Scotch Female Gallantry" showing the Prince surrounded by admiring Scots ladies, "The High Chase", or "Pursuit of the Rebels", and one depicting the Prince as Betty Burke. Engravings were also made of "The Victory over the Rebels at Culloden", and "The Fate of Rebellion", much as had been done at the close of the rebellion of 1715. Other well-known engravings include those of the Duke of Cumberland, and Miss Jenny Cameron of Glendessary. As with portraits and even miniatures, during the Victorian era many engravings were produced, particularly of Prince Charles and Flora Macdonald. The wave of Jacobite sentimentalism currently in vogue led to a whole series of romantic interpretations on canvas of events both real and imaginary, and the works of these artists were in turn converted by the engravers into a form which was cheap, highly popular, and hence readily saleable.

Essence box
    Of silver filigree, belonging to Mary of Modena, second wife of James II, and used by her at Holyrood Palace.   (SNM)

A Jacobite Legacy

Éscritoire
French, in shagreen case. A writing tablet inside, in the writing of the Prince states: "This small swess is a present from Prince Charles as a memorandum of Rannes". It also contains a silver rule, compass, and pen and pencil, and was presented by him to Andrew Hay of Rannes. The maker's name is inscribed on the rule: "Le Maire Fils, Paris." (LH)

Etching
Diamond-point, on glass, depicting James II when Duke of York. (ChC)

Étui case
Belonging to Flora Macdonald. (SNM, ERHS)

* * * * *

Additional Notes: E

A Jacobite Legacy

A Jacobite Legacy

F

Fan
 a) Of silk, adorned with the figure of Charles holding a sword, in the process of being crowned by an angel, whilst his army flees before a storm. (WHM)
 b) Of silk, showing Charles together with classical Greek figures. (RMS)
 c) Jacobite fan depicting the bust of Prince Charles, together with allegorical figures representing the three kingdoms. (DC)
 d) Sandalwood fan, with pictorial decoration, presented to Flora Macdonald in 1746, while a prisoner on parole in the house of Lady Primrose, in London. (SNM, SNE)
 e) Paper fan, decorated with the image of Prince Charles together with figures from classical Greek mythology. (PC)

Figurehead
 A large piece of wood taken from the figurehead of Le du Teillay, with a brass plaque confirming this. (PC)

Flask
  a) Drinking
   1) Discovered in Cluny's "cage". (WHM)
   2) Of pewter, found on Culloden field after the battle. (HJE)
   3) Used by Prince Charles Edward. (MnM)
  b) Powder
   French, of turned ivory, left by the Prince at Drumlanrig Castle. (DgC)
  c) Scent
   Gold-mounted scent flask belonging to Prince Henry Benedict, the Prince's brother. (CJS)

A Jacobite Legacy

Flower-stand
Of delftware, belonging to Flora. (SNM)

Flower-vase
Of salt-glazed Staffordshire stoneware, painted in coloured enamels with a portrait of Charles, and the date, 1745. (RMS)

Flute or Fife
Said to have been played during the battle of Culloden.
(SNE)

Fowling piece
Double barrelled over-and-under flintlock, by Bourdiec of Paris. The barrel is inlaid with a gold thistle beneath a crown. An inscription from Virgil's "Aeneid", so beloved of the Jacobite movement, and frequently occurring on glass, rings, and snuff mulls, is engraved on the barrel. Given to Lord Elcho by Charles, and probably originally the property of James III. (AH)

Fur
Piece of ermine fur worn by Bonnie Prince Charlie. (ERHS)

* * * * *

Additional Notes: F

A Jacobite Legacy

A Jacobite Legacy

G

Garter
 a) Pair, of coloured silk, embroidered with the rhyme: "Come let us with one heart agree To pray that God may bless P.C."
 (SNE, ERHS)
 b) Pair, with mottoes: "In God alone we put our trust" and "Our Prince is brave, his cause is just". (MJE)
 c) Single, with motto: "When this you se, remember me". (sic) Refers to James III. (MJE)
 d) Pair of garters of blue silk, embroidered with pomegranates, said to have been worn by the Prince. (SNE)
 e) Portion of a garter belonging to a Rattray clansman, who was "out" in the Forty-Five, and fought at Culloden. (SRO)
 f) Pair, of tartan silk, woven with: "God Bless PC and Down with the Rump". (JSE)
 g) Piece of, worn by Prince Charles Edward, being French, and of blue velvet lined with silk, attached to the front board of Vol III of The Lyon in Mourning by Robert Forbes. (NLS)
 h) Pair of Jacobite tartan silk garters, one reading: "When rich industry set upon our plains", the other, "Then peace and plenty cries its Stuart reigns". (ChC)

Glass
 The study of Jacobite glass is an enormous one, and only a brief outline can be given here. Most Jacobite glasses are engraved, either by diamond point or copper wheel. The former are the earlier variety, and comprise principally the rare "Amen" glasses, so called because they are engraved with two or more verses of the Jacobite national anthem, as well as the word "Amen". The wheel-engraved glasses depict the six-petalled Jacobite rose, having one or two buds on thorny stems. Where two buds are present, one will be half-open, and placed on the right side of the large rose when

A Jacobite Legacy

viewed from the front, the other closed, and placed on the left. These features possibly represent King James VIII, and his two sons. When two buds are present, a total of 4 leaves will be found on the stems, 5 where there is only one bud. Other flowers represented include forget-me-nots, daffodils, lilies-of-the-valley, carnations, honeysuckle, and sunflowers, and in addition, there may be thistles or oak leaves. Jacobite symbolism may also be expressed in the presence of moths, bees, or grubs, and sometimes in a star or compass rose. A Latin inscription of known Jacobite significance may be present, eg "Fiat"- "Let it be so", "Audentior Ibo"-"I shall go more boldly", "Revirescit"-"It grows green again". "Redi"- "Return", is sometimes engraved around the foot. Occasionally there will be reference to the particular Jacobite family who owned the glass, eg "TRAQUAIR". One variety of Jacobite glass is engraved with a portrait of Bonnie Prince Charlie in campaign dress, and these are referred to as portrait glasses. Yet another is the enamelled portrait glass, in which coloured enamels have been used to create the portrait of the Prince. A further type of glass is known, the disguised Jacobite glass, which is a glass with various elements of Jacobite symbolism, perhaps consisting of forget-me-nots, lilies, and thistles, engraved around its rim. Many Jacobite glasses have survived, especially in the case of prominent Jacobite families, who may have several in their possession. Numbers of them have been faked during the past century, and these, together with the reproduction Jacobite glass, produced without any intention to deceive, can be confusing to the collector. Perhaps the greatest controversy surrounding Jacobite glass today, centres on the period during which they were made, and Dr Seddon makes a very good case in suggesting that the majority were fabricated in the years immediately preceding, during, and after, the Forty-Five rebellion, in his excellent work, "The Jacobites and their Drinking Glasses", to which the interested reader is highly recommended for further and more detailed study. (DC, RMS, GM, PC's)

A Jacobite Legacy

Glass
   Cordial, with multiple spiral airtwist stem, from which James III drank during his last evening in Scotland. He was the guest of John Scott of Hedderwick, in Castle Place, Montrose.   (MeM)

Gloves
   a) Pair, left at Rochester by James II on the eve of his flight into exile.   (ERHS)
   b) Pair of gauntletted gloves belonging to and worn by Prince Charles, and presented by him to George Mackenzie of Delvine.   (HJE)
   c) Pair of gauntletted gloves worn on the scaffold by William Boyd, fourth Earl of Kilmarnock.   (SNM, GIE, SNE)
   d) Pair of leather gloves worn by Charles, and given by Dr Hamilton to HRH the Duke of Sussex, and subsequently bought by George, Lord Glenlyon, at the Duke's sale in 1843.   (BrC)
   e) Pair of fine leather gloves presented by the Prince to Mrs Lowthian, along with his portrait, after spending the night of 21 December 1745 at her home in High Street, Dumfries.   (PC)
   f) Pair of leather kid gloves belonging to Viscount Dundee.   (RMS)
   g) Two pairs, worn by Prince Charles.   (GIE)

Gown
   a) Of yellow brocade, worn by Margaret Boyd at the marriage of the Earl of Kilmarnock.   (GIE, SNE)
   b) Piece of the gown worn by Betty Burke.   (GIE, SNE)
   c) Piece of a gown worn by Flora Macdonald.   (DM)

Grenades
   a) Hand-, used by the grenadiers of Cumberland's army during the Forty-Five rising.   (GIE)
   b) Grenades and fuse from HMS Dartmouth.   (RMS)

A Jacobite Legacy

c) Grenades (14) thrown by the highland army into a tarn near Forest Hall, north of Kendal, on the retreat to Scotland in 1745. (LsH)

Gun
Silver-mounted, having a Spanish barrel, with inset silver plate inscribed:"C.S.1745". Presented by the Prince to Captain Macleod of Brae, Raasay, who assisted the Prince in his escape.
(HJE)

Gun lock
a) With flint, found on the field of Culloden. (HJE)
b) Another, found at Culloden. (GIE)

* * * * *

Additional Notes: G

A Jacobite Legacy

(1) Gold and agate snuffbox

(2) Interior of upper lid, with the popular Jacobite slogan,

i

(3) "Awa Whigs Awa".
Parcel gilt belt buckle, gifted by the Prince to Ian Dubh Mackinnon of Mackinnon. The supporters, a lion and leopard, are unique to the chief of Clan Mackinnon. The reverse is inscribed: "Carolus Princeps Deo Patriae Tibi".

(4) Brass and carnelian seal, with a likeness of the Prince.

(5) Wax impression (after Sir Robert Strange)

(6) Watch fob seal of gold and hawk's-eye agate, showing a rose and single bud, symbolising King James VIII and Prince Charles Edward Stuart, with, above, the motto of the Stuarts of Traquair, "Judge Nought".

(7) Detail of the above.

(8) Portrait of Prince Charles Edward after Hussey, circa 1750.

(9) Hair ring containing a sheaf of the Prince's hair.

(10) Memorial ring to Flora Macdonald

(11) Crown brooch inscribed "Do Come".

(12) Obverse side of brooch.

(13) Jacobite medals, 1712-88.

(14) Anti-Jacobite medals, 1717-46.

(15) Miniature of James Francis Edward Stuart, the Old Pretender, after Alexis Simon Belle, 1712.

(16) Snuffmull of ivory and silver, bearing the arms and motto of the distinguished Jacobite poet,

*(17) Snuffmull of ivory and ebony, belonging to the Jacobite, Alexander Smith of Longmay, dated 1745.
The inscription reads:
"Post Nubila Phabus",(sic), literally, "Sunshine After Clouds", a reference to the hoped-for restoration of the Stuarts.*

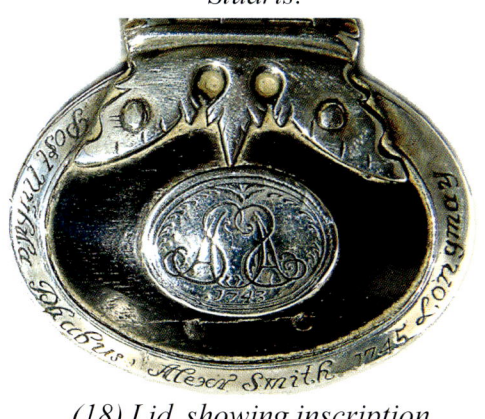

(18) Lid, showing inscription.

ix

(19) Jacobite ribbon

(20) Glass medallion depicting James VIII

(21) Silver "Amor et Spes" medal

(22) Sea Serjeants seal ring.

(23) Jacobite seal ring, "Turno Tempus Erit".

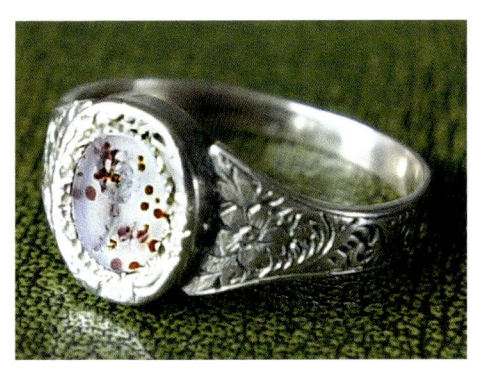

(24) Seal ring adorned with a Jacobite rose and single bud.

xi

(25) Jacobite powderhorn dated 1716, with engraved decoration including the words: "Vivat Jacobus Tertius Magna Brittaniae Rex" (sic) ie., "Long live James III, King of Great Britain".

(26) Close-up of inscription

(27) Engraving by Hogarth of Miss Jennie Cameron of Glendessary.

(28) Engraving of the Battle of Culloden, 16 April 1746, by Laurie and Whittle, 1797.

(29) Watch fob seal engraved "Redii".

(30) Engraving by Nicholas Edelinck of David's portrait of Charles at the age of 6, altered by Strange in 1745 by the addition of a bonnet and white cockade.

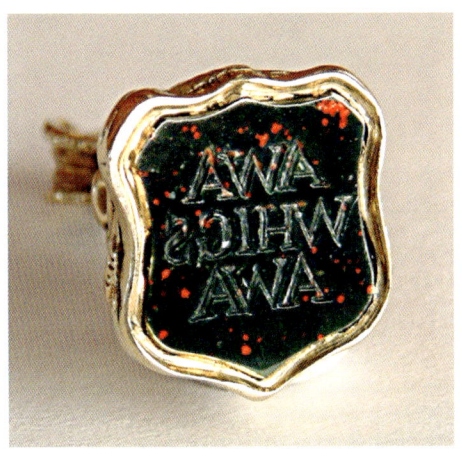

(31) Watch fob seal engraved "Awa Whigs Awa".

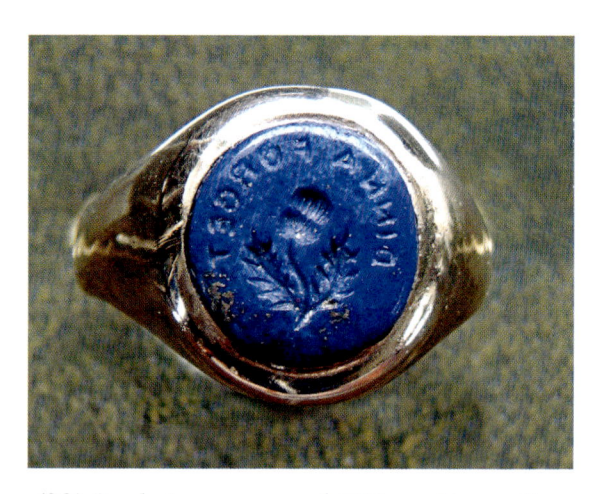

(32) Seal ring engraved "Dinna Forget"

(33) Engraving of Prince Charles Edward by Edelinck

A Jacobite Legacy

H

Habit shirt
Worn by Bonnie Prince Charlie when dressed as Betty Burke. (ERHS)

Hair, locks of
The practice of presenting locks of hair to their faithful followers was widely adhered to by the Jacobite royal family. Charles' first locks were removed at the age of 11 months, and at various times throughout childhood. The tiny amounts of hair were then mounted, usually as a sheaf, or tiny lock, either in a small glass or crystal-fronted compartment behind a portrait miniature or brooch, or in a ring or locket. The amount of hair required varies from a single strand to the considerably greater amount needed to form a plait. Six locks of the Prince's hair are associated with Flora Macdonald, but this does not necessarily call any of them into question. Bishop Forbes describes how Flora Macdonald, at the request of Mrs Macdonald of Kingsburgh, asked the Prince for a lock of his hair. He allowed her to remove the lock, which she then divided between herself and Mrs Macdonald.

1) Gold locket with double-sided glass containing the hair of James VIII, Clementina, Charles and Henry. The reverse engraved: "Hair of James (son of James VII) of his consort and their sons Charles Edward and Henry". Also "Francis Farquarson of Monaltrie, 1745".
(ERHS)

2) Silver brooch containing a lock of Prince Charles' hair, in a paste mount. The front shows the figure of Aphrodite riding in a shell chariot, drawn by two horse-like sea creatures. An inscription at the back reads: "A lock of Prince Charles Edward's hair cut 1763". (FCS, CJS, PC)

A Jacobite Legacy

3) Beaded box containing a lock of Prince Charles's hair.　(TH)
4) Lock of hair of James VIII.　(TH)
5) Lock of Clementina's hair.　(TH)
6) Lock of Bonnie Prince Charlie's hair in a silver case.　(WHM)
7) Lock of the Prince's hair belonging to Flora. (HJE, WHM)
8) Lock of Bonnie Prince Charlie's hair.　(WHM)
9) Locks of the Prince's hair, with other relics.　(RS)
10) Lock of the Prince's hair.　(CJS)
11) Christening locket with a lock of the Prince's hair. (CJS)
12) Stickpin containing a lock of the Prince's hair.　(CJS)
13) Lock of the Prince's hair in a wooden frame.　(GM)
14) Gold locket containing a lock of the Prince's hair, with "C P" embroidered on the white silk background.　(HP)
15) Pearl brooch containing locks of the Prince's & Flora's hair.　(ERHS)
16) Gold locket with the hair of the Prince and Flora on opposite sides.　(ERHS)
17) Gold ring with a lock of the Prince's hair.　(ERHS)
18) Gold locket with a miniature of the Prince, and a lock of his hair at the rear.　(ERHS)
19) Gold locket with the locks of hair of James, Clementina, Charles & Henry.　(ERHS)
20) Lock of Charles' hair, presented by him to Flora. (ERHS)
21) Lock of Charles' hair, in a frame with other relics. (ERHS)
22) Lock of Charles' hair.　(ERHS)
23) Lock of Charles' hair, in a frame with a portion of his Garter ribbon.　(ERHS)
24) Lock of Charles' hair.　(ERHS)
25) Crystal locket containing a lock of Charles' hair. (ERHS)
26) Lock of Charles' hair at age 12.　(ERHS)
27) Lock of Charles' hair aged 16.　(ERHS, GIE)

A Jacobite Legacy

28) Lock of Charles' hair. (ERHS)
29) Diamond brooch with a lock of Charles' hair. (ERHS)
30) Lock of Prince James' hair. (ERHS)
31) Gold ring with the monogram "CPR", and a lock of Charles' hair. (ERHS)
32) Prayer ring containing a lock of the Prince's hair. (ERHS)
33) Gold ring with a lock of Prince Charles' hair, engraved beneath: "Mêche de cheveux de Prince Charles Edward Stuart 1744". (PC)
34) Miniature of Bonnie Prince Charlie, mounted with a tiny lock of his hair. (DC)
35) Case containing a lock of Charles' hair, said to have been cut after his death. (HJE)
36) Hair of James II and his son, James Francis Edward. (SNM)
37) Oblong medallion containing the hair of the Prince, along with part of his Garter ribbon. (SNM)
38) Gold oval pendant locket, with a glazed compartment containing a lock of Charles' hair, inscribed "Lock of Prince Charles Edward Stuart's hair, 1763". (FCS)
39) Gold ring with a lock of the Prince's hair. (SNM)
40) Locket containing a lock of Charles' hair, and a piece of his Garter ribbon. (BrC)
41) Lock of Charles' hair, with a letter stating; "Got from HRH Aug 3 1737, when it was cut off". (BrC)
42) Lock of Charles' hair in a hair ring, together with a piece of his plaid, and a note reading: "I Got from Gask". (BrC)
43) Lock of Lord George Murray's hair. (BrC)
44) Lock of Lady Amelia Murray's hair, in a mourning ring. (BrC)
45) Lock of Charles' hair in a gold ring set with crystal, engraved: "Love and Honour", with Prince of Wales' feathers, a thistle, and rose, presented by him to Flora. (CDhM)

A Jacobite Legacy

46) Lock of the Prince's hair. (CDhM, RSSE)
47) Lock of Charles' hair, plaited under crystal in a gold ring. (TBM)
48) Lock of the Prince's hair in a gold memorial ring, inscribed: "Prince Charles Edward Stuart, 1788." (PC)
49) Lock of the Prince's hair, given by Cardinal Henry to James Byers of Tonley, Aberdeenshire. (SNE)
50) Lock of the Prince's hair, contained in a brooch. (SNE)
51) Lock of the Prince's hair, in a diamond locket, given by him to John Kinloch of Kinry. (SNE)
52) Lock of Charles' hair, contained in a blue enamel marquise ring. (SNE)
53) Two locks of Charles' hair, in a locket worn by the Prince, and given by him to James Carnegie of Boysack. (SNE)
54) Lock of Charles' hair, contained in a heart-shaped locket, under crystal. (WRS)
55) Lock of Charles' hair, in a diamond ring. (WRS)
56) Lock of Flora Macdonald's hair, plaited under crystal, together with that of her husband, Allan Macdonald of Kingsburgh, in a gold mourning ring. Flora died in 1790. (PC)
57) Lock of Charles' hair. (IM)
58) Lock of Charles' hair, in the glazed compartment of a jabot pin. (IM)
59) Lock of Charles' hair, in the form of a long plait, cut when aged 16. (IM)
60) Lock of Flora Macdonald's hair, contained in a pendant. (IM)
61) Locks of Flora's and Charles' hair, in a ring. (IM)
62) Lock of Charles' hair, in a pendant. (IM)
63) Lock of hair of James VIII. (SRO)
64) Lock of Charles' hair, belonging originally to Sir John Stanley, who was in the diplomatic service in Rome after 1745. (JSE)

A Jacobite Legacy

65) Lock of Charles' plaited hair in a gold ring. (CE)
66) Lock of Charles' hair in a highland brooch. (GIE)
67) Lock of Charles' hair cut at age 16, in a contemporary silver locket ringed with garnets. (ChC)
68) Lock of Charles' hair in a brooch, clipped by Flora Macdonald, the other half given by her to Mrs Macdonald of Kingsburgh. (HJE)
69) Single strand of Charles' hair. (WHM)
70) Lock of the Prince's hair, cut in 1737, and given by Lord James Murray to Dr Watson. (WC, WHM)
71) Lock of King James VIII's hair, contained in a gold locket, with "JR8" in gold wire, the back inscribed: "Gift Ld Huntly to Jno Grant, 1801". (RMS)
72) Lock of Henry Benedict's hair. (EDC)
73) Lock of Queen Clementina Sobieska's hair. (EDC)
74) Lock of King James VIII's hair. (EDC)
75) Lock of King James VII's hair. (EDC)
76) Large lock of the Prince's hair, cut at age 16, and framed together with a silver "Micat Inter Omnes" medal. (EDC)
77) Lock of hair of Donald Macdonald of Kinlochmoidart, contained in a memorial ring inscribed in the loop: "Donald McDonald (sic) of Kinlochmoidart, suffered October 18, 1746, for King and Country". (CDdM)

Halberd
Left behind at Naworth Castle, near Brampton, by the highland army, when billeted there in 1745, along with a javelin and pike. (NC)

Handkerchief
Formerly belonging to Charlotte, the Prince's daughter, and stained with her tears. It is said to have been given by Charles in lieu of wages, along with a lace collar and ruffles. (WHM)

A Jacobite Legacy

Helmet
Portion of, belonging to James Graham of Claverhouse, killed at the Battle of Killiecrankie in 1690. The helmet was removed from his grave around 1794. (SNM)

High chair
Of oak, used by the infant James VI. (SNM)

* * * * *

Additional Notes: H

A Jacobite Legacy

A Jacobite Legacy

I

Intaglio
Glass, depicting a likeness of Prince Charles Edward Stuart.
(FCS)

Invitation card
To a meeting of the Society of Sea Serjeants at Swansea, June 7th, 1749. Decorated with the star and dolphin emblems of the society. (WRS)

* * * * *

Additional Notes: I

A Jacobite Legacy

J

Jacket
a) Of tartan, belonging to Bonnie Prince Charlie. (ERHS)
b) Of hard tartan, made in Uist, and worn at Culloden.
(WHM)

Javelin
Left behind by the highland army when billeted at Naworth Castle, Brampton, in 1745, along with a pike and halberd. (NC)

Jewel   (See also under Badge)
a) Of the Cycle. Of coloured enamels set in gold and surmounted by a diamond bow. On the face the Jewel is inscribed: "LADY WILLIAMS WYNN. LADY PATRONESS-ELECTED 1780". At the back, on a royal blue disc surrounded by oak leaves: "INSTITUTED JUNE Ye 10th 1710". In a shagreen case. (WRS)
b) Of the Order of the Thistle, belonging formerly to James Drummond, IVth Earl of Perth. It is of gold, with the figure of St Andrew on one side, and a thistle on the other.   (SNM)

Jug
a) In which cream was served to the Prince at Gortleg House.
(HJE)
b) Pair, used by the Cycle Club, decorated with white roses and thistles, and inscribed: "Fiat".   (WRS)
c) Saltglazed stoneware jug with a portrait of the Prince, and a tartan border near the rim.   (BM)
d) Of silver, formerly belonging to Flora Macdonald.
(NCDCR)
e) Stoneware, decorated with a naïve portrait of the Prince in campaign dress, with a butterfly and rose. Mid-18th century.
(PW)

* * * * *

A Jacobite Legacy

Additional Notes: J

A Jacobite Legacy

K

Keg
Carried by Hugh Chisholm of Fasnakyle while acting as guide to the Prince in Upper Strathglass. (HJE)

Key
a) Of Culloden Castle, handed to Prince Charles by the Lord President's steward. (HJE)
b) Found in a field, and thought to have been discarded by Jacobite fugitives. (IM)

Kilt
Piece of kilt worn by Bonnie Prince Charlie. (WHM)

Kit-fiddle (?)
Belonging to Sir John Cope, and taken at the Battle of Prestonpans by Robert Robertson of Moulin. (SNE)

Knife
a) With ivory grip, said to have been taken from the side of a horse on the field of Culloden. (BrC)
b) Knife, of skene-ochles type, said to have belonged to the Prince. (MnM)
c) Of small dimensions, used by the Prince whilst in the Glenmoriston area. (SNE)
d) Pocket-knife said to have belonged to the Prince. (IM)
e) Steel knife with silver-mounted agate handle, taken from the Prince's baggage after Culloden. (ChC)

* * * * *

A Jacobite Legacy

Additional Notes: K

A Jacobite Legacy

L

Ladle
Silver, formerly belonging to Flora Macdonald. (NCDCR)

Lance
Found on the field of Prestonpans, 1745. (GIE)

Lancet
and wooden mallet, used by the Hanoverian veterinary surgeon to bleed horses in 1745-46. (HJE)

Linen
Table, used by the Prince whilst staying at the home of Mrs Lowthian, in High Street, Dumfries, on 21 December 1745. (PC)

Lining
Fragment of the silk lining of the coat worn by Charles Radcliffe, the Earl of Derwentwater, on the scaffold in 1716.
(WC, ChC)

Lists
a) Contemporary list of persons from Glen Urquart who were "out" in the Forty-Five, and subsequently surrendered to Ludovic Grant of Grant. (HJE)
b) Similar list of persons from Glenmoriston. (HJE)
c) Of the killed or wounded, of the Stewarts of Appin and their followers. (HJE)
d) Of those subscribing to a fund for the relief of prisoners at Carlisle. (DC)
e) Cycle list, pasted on wood, and varnished, attached to a Cycle button. (WRS)
f) Cycle list for the year 1721-22, written on card, and including the name of Sir Watkin Williams Wynn. (ChC)

A Jacobite Legacy

Lithograph
 Of banknotes, printed by Sir D Y Cameron in 1928, from the copper plate fabricated by Robert Strange at Inverness in 1746, these are notes for One Penny, Two Pence, Three Pence, and Six Pence, and were never issued. (SNE, WHM, G-WC)

Locket
  a) Christening
   Containing a lock of Bonnie Prince Charlie's infant hair.
                                                      (CJS)
  b) Crystal
   Containing a lock of Bonnie Prince Charlie's hair, given by him to Miss Dolbin in 1745. (ERHS, GIE)
  c) Diamond,
   Containing a lock of the Prince's hair, given by him to John Kinloch of Kinry. (SNE)
  d) Enamel and gold
   Depicting Flora Macdonald weeping before a tomb. (ERHS)
  e) Gold
   1) Containing the hair locks of the Prince and Flora on opposite sides. (ERHS)
   2) Containing a miniature of the Prince aged one, set with rubies, diamonds, and emeralds, with a lock of his hair at the rear.
                                                      (ERHS)
   3) Containing locks of hair belonging to James, Clementina, Charles, and Henry. Inscribed: "Francis Farquharson of Monaltrie, 1745", and "Hair of JAMES, son of KING JAMES VII) of his Consort and their sons, CHARLES EDWARD & HENRY."
                                                      (ERHS)
   4) With a portrait of the Prince at the age of about 45, given by him to Mrs Murray of Broughton. (ERHS)
   5) Containing a miniature of the Prince, presented to Miss Pedder at a ball given at Preston on 27 November 1745.
       (Illustration, Culloden and the '45, by J Black.)

A Jacobite Legacy

6) Oval pendant locket containing a lock of the Prince's hair, inscribed: "Lock of Prince Charles Edward Stuart's hair, 1763". (FCS)

7) Containing a lock of the Prince's hair, and a piece of his Garter ribbon. (BrC)

8) Of heart shape, containing a lock of the Prince's hair under crystal. (WRS)

9) Containing a lock of the Prince's hair, and "C P" embroidered on the white silk background. (HP)

10) Having a portrait of Prince James on one side, and the royal arms of Scotland on the other. (ERHS)

11) Containing a portrait of Francis Charteris, 7th Earl of Wemyss, and husband of Lady Katherine Gordon. (JSE)

12) Containing a portrait of Charles Edward Stewart, with the monogram: "CE". (GIE)

13) Set with pearls and garnets, and containing a lock of Charles' hair, cut at age 17. (PC)

14) Containing a lock of King James VIII's hair, with "JR8" in gold wire, the back inscribed: "Gift Ld Huntly to Jno Grant, 1802".

f) Memorial

Containing the locks of hair of two dead sons of Flora Macdonald, Ranald and Alexander. (SNM)

g) Rock crystal and gold, set with diamonds, rubies and emeralds, containing a portrait of Bonnie Prince Charlie. (ERHS)

h) Silver

1. Containing a lock of Prince Charles' hair, formerly belonging to Flora Macdonald. (HJE)

2. Engraved with an anchor flanked by a heart in flame, and another pierced by an arrow, Jacobite symbols of steadfastness and mourning. (JSE)

3. Containing a lock of Charles' hair cut at age 16, the contemporary locket set with garnets. (ChC)

A Jacobite Legacy

i) Worn by the Prince, and given by him to James Carnegie of Boysack. Now contains two locks of the Prince's hair. (SNE)

* * * * *

Additional Notes: L

A Jacobite Legacy

M

Mantle
a) Of the Order of the Thistle, which belonged to James Drummond, IVth Earl of Perth, who was imprisoned in 1688, and subsequently joined James VII at St Germain-en-Laye. (SNM)
b) Fragment of the white satin mantle belonging to Clementina, together with its red silk lining, and worn by her when she received the last sacrament. (WC, ChC)

Mantle chain
Belonging to Princess Louise of Stolberg. (SNM)

Manuscript sheet
Of music, which, when folded in a certain way, conveyed a secret message to the Prince: "Conceal yourself, your foes look for you". (SNM, GIE)

Maps
These consist principally, of battle plans of the three major battles fought during the Rebellion, Prestonpans, sometimes referred to as Tranent or Gladsmuir, Falkirk, and Culloden. Maps are also in existence showing the details of the troop disposals at the skirmish of Clifton Bridge, near Penrith. Other maps of interest include road maps produced by Ordnance after 1746, showing the new military roads, maps drawn after the Forty-Five indicating the route taken by the Prince and his army in their marches through Scotland, and a map showing the territory occupied by each clan, together with an estimate of the number of men who could be raised by each chief. (NLS, RMS, H.M. the Queen)
a) Map of Great Britain in 1746, by John Finlayson, showing the route taken by the highland army through England and Scotland.

A Jacobite Legacy

Finlayson was himself enlisted in the highland army, and was briefly imprisoned after the Forty-Five. (TH)
    b) Another Finlayson map. (RMS)

Marriage certificate
    a) Of James VIII and Clementina Sobieska. (ERHS)
    b) Of Flora Macdonald and Allan Macdonald of Kingsburgh. (A)

Mast
    Fragment of mast of boat provided by Ian Dubh Mackinnon to convey the Prince from Skye to Morar, on July 4, 1746. (DC)

Medal
    a) Silver Oak Society medal, formerly belonging to Donald Robertson of Woodshiel. (CDhM)
    b) Bronze medal of Pope Pius VII, 1804, contained in a leather case, and formerly belonging to Henry, Cardinal York.

Medallion
  a) Portrait
    1) A plaster medallion of Prince Charles Edward. (FCS)
    2) A paste medallion of Andrew Lumisden by Tassie. (SNM, SNPG)
    3) A porcelain medallion of Clementina. (ERHS)
    4) Two, of porcelain, depicting the obverse and reverse of Filipo Cropanese's medal to commemorate the death of James III in 1766. (ChC)
    5) Ivory medallion of James III. (WRS)
    6) Silver, showing the head of Charles Edward, with the words: "Carolus Walliae Princeps, 1745", similar to the "Amor et Spes" medal of 1748, but with no reverse, and presented by him to his ADC, William Home of Broomhouse. (SNE, CE)

A Jacobite Legacy

7) Plaster medallion of Charles Edward Stuart in profile, mounted in a wooden frame. (TH)
8) Tassie medallion of James III. (ChC)
9) Tassie medallion of Andrew Lumisden, dated 1784. (ChC)
10) Glass medallion or cliché by Ottone Hamerani, depicting the obverse side of his medal commemorating the proxy marriage of James III to Clementina, in 1719. The reverse is blank. See also token. (PC)
11) Portrait medallion of Queen Clementina, of ivory, and mounted in an ebony frame. (WC)
b) Of black steel, a gift of the Prince, together with a necklace and cross, and a bracelet. (ERHS)
c) Oblong medallion containing the hair of Bonnie Prince Charlie, and part of the Garter worn by him. (SNM, GIE)

Medals

These, together with portraits, miniatures, and engravings, were the propaganda of their day, and provide a fascinating insight into the entire Jacobite movement. Essentially, they were exercises in public relations, enabling the exiled Jacobite court to keep its cause ever alive through the eyes of its followers. These medals would be issued for sale, or presented to adherents, keeping them abreast of each significant event in the Jacobite calendar, acting as a very useful and important means of publicity. However, side by side with the production of medals by the Jacobite court in St Germain-en-Laye and in Rome, was the issue of anti-Jacobite medals by the Williamites, and later, the Hanoverians, so that making a study of the medals of the period, exposes the researcher to the whole history of the Jacobite movement. Normally, these medals are constructed of silver, gold, or bronze. They commence at the genesis of the movement in 1688, with the issue of a medal to commemorate the birth of James Francis Edward in that year, and

A Jacobite Legacy

end, 100 years later, with a medal issued by the Hanoverians on the centenary of the Glorious Revolution. The many momentous events occurring between these dates were almost always marked by the issue of a medal. The first produced on behalf of the Williamites, was that commemorating the acceptance of the throne by William III, also minted in 1688. The victorious battles of the Rebellion of 1715, Sheriffmuir and Preston, were minted by I Croker for George I, whilst, on the Jacobite side, the escape of Clementina from Innsbruck, the marriage of James III, and the birth of Charles, were all the subjects of medals, and were products of the famous Hamerani family of medalists, who were working in Rome. The issue of a medal in 1731 of the two young princes was felt to be an important publicity measure, but George II responded with a medal depicting his own two children. The landing in Scotland of Prince Charles on July 23, 1745, and his subsequent occupation of Edinburgh, are followed by a whole series of anti-Jacobite medals: the Recapture of Carlisle, the Retreat to Scotland, the Culloden Medal, and several commemorating the Defeat of the Rebels. Some interesting Jacobite medals occur after this period, with the issue of the "Amor et Spes" medal in 1748 in protest against the Anglo-French Treaty of Aix-La-Chapelle", and the "Look, Love, and Follow" medal, both minted by CN Roettier. Each side sought to mark any event of importance by the issue of a medal, so that, on the Jacobite side, medals were issued to commemorate the death of James' sister, Princess Louisa in 1712, and the marriage of Charles and Louise of Stolberg in 1772. A medal was issued in 1735 with the death of Clementina, whilst that of her husband, James, was commemorated in a medal of 1766. On the Hanoverian side, medals were released to celebrate their perceived victory at Sheriffmuir in 1715, and the return of the victor of Culloden to London after the capture of Carlisle. Both sides issued medals after the attempted rising of 1708. Other medals released by the Jacobites include the Oak Society and Cycle Club medals, as well

A Jacobite Legacy

as "touch pieces", used by James as well as Charles in the treatment of scrofula, otherwise known as the King's Evil. The last Jacobite medal minted was following the death of Charles in 1788. The inscription on the obverse reads, in Latin: "Henry IX, King of Great Britain, France and Ireland, Defender of the Faith, Cardinal Bishop of Tusculum." (RMS, GM, TM, WHM, DC, etc)

Medicine chest

This item is a travelling set of medical remedies belonging to Prince Charles, contained in a mahogany carrying case, complete with small scales and weights and measures. It was entrusted to Charles' physician, Sir Stuart Threipland. (RMS)

Miniatures

These constitute fascinating items of memorabilia, and refer to both the Jacobite royal family, and to members of the Jacobite aristocracy. James III and his spouse, Clementina Sobieska, were both represented in miniatures, as were their children, Charles and Henry. These likenesses were reproduced throughout their lifetimes, and were a convenient way of keeping the Jacobite royal family in the public eye. Miniatures made very useful gifts, and many Jacobite families owned several of these images, from infancy to adult life. Sometimes a lock of hair could be inserted at the rear, thus making the object even more personal. A great number of miniatures of Prince Charles Edward has survived, sometimes with a silver and paste mount. Others are mounted on lockets or rings, or on the lids of snuffboxes or bonbonnières, occasionally on the surface of a second, or "secret" lid. One, of Louise of Stolberg, Charles' wife, has been mounted within a badge of the Order of St Andrew. Another depicts Charles as a tiny infant. Many portraits in miniature of the Prince were copied from other, larger, paintings, and distributed amongst his followers. Some were copied by miniaturists from an engraving by Sir Robert Strange, showing the Prince in

A Jacobite Legacy

campaign dress, facing to his right, and wearing a blue bonnet with white cockade, with the Star and Ribbon of the Garter on his breast, and the badge of the Order of St Andrew around his neck. The miniatures were usually on ivory, and were seldom signed. Occasionally a signature, such as that of Zincke, or Kamme, will be found. Signed miniatures of Prince Charles Edward include those by Marolles, and Hayman, who also painted a miniature of Flora Macdonald, while an artist named V Stern painted a miniature of Prince Henry Benedict, Duke of York, in 1743. The miniaturist Benjamin Arlaud painted a likeness of James Francis Edward, which can be seen in Traquair House, while other miniaturists copied a well-known likeness of the monarch clad in armour, painted in 1712 by Alexis Simon Belle. One of these was Belle's wife, Anne Chéron. Rosalba Carriera executed charming miniatures of Charles, as well as of his mother Clementina, the latter of particularly outstanding quality. Other miniatures exist of many prominent Jacobites, as, for example, William, Marquis of Tullibardine, the Jacobite Duke of Atholl, and are preserved by their descendants.

Mirror
    a) Of giltwood with painted glass frame, inscribed: "The Mirror Prince Charles Edward used in his camp equipage at Culloden". (JSE)
    b) Belonging to Lord Ogilvie. (GIE)

Mitre
    Of white damask, in a leather case bearing the Royal Arms, with cardinal's hat above, formerly belonging to Cardinal York.
    (SNM, PC)

Mittens
    a) Pair of long white mittens worn by the Prince at the last Holyrood Ball, embroidered in blue silk with the words: "God Preserve Prince Charles". (ERHS)

A Jacobite Legacy

b) Pair of mittens used by the Prince when disguised as Betty Burke. (ERHS)

Model
Ship's, of the government sloop Hazard, which was captured by the highland army in November, 1745, and renamed The Prince Charles. The vessel, of 270 tons, ran aground at the Kyle of Tongue in March, 1746, following a sea chase. (DC)

Moneybox
Of oak and walnut, bound with brass, and of continental manufacture. Reputed to have belonged to Prince Charles, and left behind in Drumlanrig Castle on the retreat northwards.
(DgC, GIE)

Mortar
Of marble, from Culloden House. (HJE)

Mug
a) Porcelain mug, of 1st period Worcester, with a portrait of Bonnie Prince Charlie. (CJS)

b) Of Jackfield ware, marked: "Twenty-Seven". Used by a member of the Lloyd family of Montgomery at meetings of the local Jacobite club, where each member was known only by a number. (WRS)

c) Of earthenware, commemorating Charles Edward Stuart, and inscribed: "The Escape of Bonnie Prince Charlie". (DyM)

d) Of Chinese export porcelain, depicting Charles Edward Stuart. Circa 1745. (BM)

e) Of Chinese export porcelain, depicting William, Duke of Cumberland, and commemorating his victory at Culloden. Circa 1746. (BM)

f) Of delftware, with a portrait of the Duke of Cumberland, inscribed: "Samuel and Mary Pledge 1748". (BM)

A Jacobite Legacy

g) English saltglaze pint mug, circa 1745, inscribed in scratch-blue with a Jacobite poem. (ChC)

h) Of Jackfield ware, bearing in gold a likeness of the Prince in highland dress, and adorned with thistles. (ChC)

Musket

a) Flintlock musket found on the battlefield at Falkirk. (CJS)
b) Of Continental manufacture, with Jacobite inscriptions. (CJS)

* * * * *

Additional Notes: M

A Jacobite Legacy

A Jacobite Legacy

N

Nails
Of iron, recovered from the wreck of La Fine. (MeM)

Napkin
Of damask, bearing the maker's name: "John Ochiltree, Weaver in Edinburgh, 1712", and the armorial bearings of George Seton, fifth Earl of Winton, whose estate was forfeited in 1716.
(SNM)

Neck slide
Of gold, with "IR God Save the King", in gold wire under crystal. (RMS)

Necklace
a) Pearl, with 57 freshwater pearls, belonging to Jean Gordon, wife of the 2nd Duke of Perth. (SNM)
b) With a cross, the gift of Prince Charles, together with a medallion of black steelwork and a bracelet. (ERHS)
c) Enamelled, consisting of a garland of white roses supporting a pendant containing a miniature of the Prince, surmounted by a crown. (IM)

Needlecase
a) Of ivory, belonging to Flora Macdonald. (WHM)
b) Silver needlecase with three compartments, engraved with Prince of Wales' feathers, and "Fingask Castle". (FCS)
c) Silver needlecase used by Flora Macdonald.
(SNM, ERHS, HJE)

Nutmeg grater   See under Canteen

* * * * *

A Jacobite Legacy

Additional Notes: N

A Jacobite Legacy

O

Oatcake
 "A piece of cake found in a Highlander's pocket on the field of Culloden the day of the battle. R. Chambers." Later belonging to Sir Walter Scott. (A)

* * * * *

Additional Notes: O

A Jacobite Legacy

P

Painting, anamorphic
This type of painting is a disguised portrait of Bonnie Prince Charlie. At first sight the painting appears to be a blur of formless colours, but on placing a polished wood or mirrored cylinder on top of the horizontal surface, the distortion is corrected, and the Prince's likeness appears on the cylinder. (WHM, FCS, CJS)

Panel
Of green velvet, bearing the arms of Henry Benedict as Cardinal York, worked in gold and silver threads and coloured silks. His royal arms are surmounted by a cardinal's hat. (JSE)

Panelling
Oak, from Exeter House, where the Prince stayed whilst in Derby. (DyM)

Paper-knife
Constructed from a piece of the timbers of La Fine. (MeM)

Pendant
a) Of gold, enamel, and pearls, formerly belonging to Mary Queen of Scots, and later to Flora Macdonald. (HJE)
b) With strands of Flora's and Charles' hair. (IM)
c) Containing a lock of Charles' hair. (IM)
d) Gold, containing a verse lamenting the death of William III. (RMS)
e) Silver, depicting Duncan Forbes of Culloden, dated 1747. (CE)
f) With garnets and diamonds, containing a lock of Charles' hair, and the letters "C P" in gold script. (IM)
g) Containing a plaited lock of Flora Macdonald's hair. (IM)

A Jacobite Legacy

Peppermill
    Belonging to Bonnie Prince Charlie.   (WHM)

Pewter
    a) Miscellaneous, from Culloden House.   (HJE)
    b) Large dinner service, inscribed with a ducal coronet, and so used as evidence against Lord Lovat at his trial.   (HJE)
    c) Drinking flask, found on Culloden field after the battle.
    (HJE)

Pin
    a) Gold, in a piece of Prince Charles' plaid or kilt, given by him to Lady Mackintosh a day or two before Culloden.
    (SNM, GIE)
    b) Larding   See under Cutlery.
    c) Plaid, of bronze, in the shape of a broadsword, found on Culloden field in 1850.   (HJE)

Pince-nez
    In case, belonging to Cardinal York.   (SNM)

Pincushion
    Two distinct types of Jacobite pincushion can be recognised. The first type is made of white satin, with blue tassels at each corner. The cushion itself is printed with blue lettering with, in the centre, a Jacobite rose, surrounded by the words: "Mart For King and Cou 1746", and a list of many of those executed after the defeat of the rebellion. The second type of pincushion usually consists of embroidered silks, sometimes with a Jacobite text, as, "God Bless P.C." Another reads: "Down with the rump. Preserve KJ; PC; DH; for ever". Both types were worked by Jacobite ladies, although there is a suggestion that the former were made to commemorate the first centenary of the '45 Rising.
    a) White satin with blue corner tassels. The names of the

A Jacobite Legacy

executed Jacobites are printed on both sides in blue, around a central white rose, and the legend: "Mart:For:King and Cou:1746". (PC)

    b) 3 similar. (CJS)
    c) 3 similar. (ERHS)
    d) Similar. (MJE)
    e) Similar. (WRS, JSE)
    f) Similar. (SNM)
    g) Similar. (ChC)
    h) Similar. (MM)

    i) Jacobite pincushion with "God Bless P.C. and down with the rump" embroidered on the attached ribbon. Executed in blue, green, cream, and brown silks. (CJS)

    j) Jacobite pincushion formerly belonging to Miss Dolbin, to whom Charles had presented a crystal locket containing a lock of his hair. (ERHS, GIE)

    k) Pincushion embroidered "God Bless P C". (HP)

    l) Pincushion, with pendant ribbon, embroidered with the words: "Liberty-Property-No Excise-Down with the Rump". (WRS)

    m) Pincushion with attached tartan silk ribbon woven with the words: "God Preserve PC and Down with the Rump". (JSE)

    n) Pincushion worked in silk, the cushion with the words: "Down with the Rump", its ribbon: "God Preserve P.C. for Ever". (ChC)

Pike
    Left behind by the highland army whilst billeted at Naworth Castle, Brampton, in 1745, along with a javelin and halberd. (NC)

Pipe
    Portion of, belonging to Charles. (BrC)

A Jacobite Legacy

Pipestopper
Of bronze, decorated with a portrait of the Jacobite doctor, Henry Sacheverell. (ChC)

Pistols
Pistols may be designated as Jacobite when reputed to have been found or excavated from the battlefields of Prestonpans, Falkirk, or Culloden. A collection of such pistols, found at Culloden, is preserved at Moy Hall, and other, single pistols, exist in both private and museum collections. Pistols originally owned by known Jacobites also fall into this category. Amongst them is a flintlock all-steel pistol with ramshorn butt, by the renowned Doune gunsmith, Thomas Caddell, reputedly owned by Colonel John Roy Stewart, the commander of the Edinburgh Regiment of the highland army during the Forty-Five. Another, of snaphaunce construction, was presented by Prince Charles to his secretary, John Murray of Broughton, who later turned King's evidence crucial to the conviction and execution of Simon Fraser of Lovat. Two pairs of French pistols were presented by him to James Edgar, secretary to the Old Pretender. One of these, having over-and-under barrels, and signed H Muet Lejeune, is said to have been worn by Charles at the battle of Culloden. Two single pistols, the first by Daniel L Walker of Dumbarton, the second by Alexander Campbell of Doune, were presented by the Prince to Donald Macdonell of Lochgarry and Donald Cameron of Lochiel respectively, both of whom escaped to France with him, aboard the French ship, L'Heureux. To the latter he also presented a pair of pistols after the defeat at Culloden. A further pair of all-steel pistols with ramshorn butts, by the Doune gunsmith John Murdoch, is adorned with Charles' cypher, and was reputedly presented by him to the Master of Sinclair on the occasion of his joining the army as a gentleman volunteer. Still in existence is a pair of French walnut-stocked pistols marked "Allevin, Paris", believed to have been Charles' personal

A Jacobite Legacy

property. Other pairs of pistols were presented by the Prince to James Stirling of Craigbarnet, Robert Strange, and one Anthony Swymmer, whilst among the many pistols formerly in the possession of notable Jacobites, are those of Macdonald of Kingsburgh, Macdonald of Glenaladale, Lord Panmure, John Graham of Claverhouse, and Rob Roy Macgregor, the last of whom, along with Lord Panmure, took part in the 1715 Rising. Another pair, all-steel flintlock pistols by Segalas, London, belonged to a Hanoverian officer who was captured at Prestonpans. The present whereabouts of many of these pistols is unknown. A number were exhibited at the Exhibition of the Royal House of Stuart, which took place in 1889 at the New Gallery in Regent Street, London. Many were displayed in 1903 at the Highland and Jacobite Exhibition in Inverness, and some remain in private collections.

Plaid (See also Tartan)
  a) Piece of the Prince's plaid, left by him at Moy Hall. (MH)
  b) Of silk, belonging to Bonnie Prince Charlie. (ERHS)
  c) Of hard tartan, belonging to Bonnie Prince Charlie.
   (WHM)
  d) Found on Culloden field after the battle, together with a silver plaid brooch in it. 17th century. (HJE)
  e) Piece of tartan plaid worn by the Prince. (HJE)
  f) Piece of tartan plaid given by the Prince to Duncan Mackintosh, who fought at Culloden. (HJE)
  g) Piece of Charles' plaid, divided amongst the chiefs after Culloden. (HJE)
  h) Worn by the Prince, and taken from his shoulders and given out of gratitude to a farmer's wife who had given him protection after Culloden. (SNM)
  i) Piece of Charles' plaid, together with a lock of his hair in a hair ring, with a note: "I Got from Gask". (BrC)
  j) A piece of Charles' plaid worn on his arrival at Moy Hall.
   (BrC)

A Jacobite Legacy

k) Fragment of plaid given by the Prince to Mrs Robertson of Lude. (CDhM)

l) Piece of the Prince's plaid, along with a portion of his tobacco pipe. (BrC)

m) Piece of the Prince's plaid containing a gold pin, and given by him to Lady Macintosh. (SNM, ERHS, GIE)

n) Piece of plaid worn by Charles on the night before the battle of Culloden. (ERHS)

o) Piece of the Prince's plaid from Moy Hall, together with a note reading: "A piece of the plaid worn by the Prince/Pretender the day before the Battle of Culloden. He left it at Moy Hall, and this piece was cut off and given me by Lady Mackintosh". Dated August 1826. (IM)

p) Piece of the Prince's plaid from Moy Hall. (PE1)

q) Piece of the Prince's plaid from Moy Hall. (BeC)

r) Tartan plaid said to have been worn by the Prince. (SNE)

s) Portion of plaid worn by Fraser of Struie at Culloden. (SNE)

t) Piece of tartan plaid from Moy Hall. (SRO)

u) Tartan plaid, of Stuart tartan, presented by the Prince to Mrs Graham of Ellerton Grange, near Southwaite, Carlisle, where the Prince stayed on the retreat northwards. (THM)

v) Portion of the Prince's plaid, together with a letter from him to Sir James Kinloch, inviting him to join the standard. (RMS)

w) Portion of tartan plaid worn by the Prince. (GIE)

x) Plaid worn by Prince Charles Edward Stuart whilst a guest of Lady Elizabeth Stuart, Lady Primrose, in London in 1750. (EDC)

Plait

Of Charles' hair, cut off at the age of 16, and since preserved by the Earls of Carnwath. (IM)

A Jacobite Legacy

Plaque
    a) Memorial
        1) with the names of 19 Jacobite martyrs.   (MJE)
        2) with the names of 73 Jacobite martyrs.   (MJE)
        3) in the form of a five-petalled rose, with the names of 35 Jacobite martyrs. The names of Charles and Henry, and their dates of birth, are placed at the edges of the petals.   (MJE)
    b) Gold on bronze, of Prince Charles in highland dress.   (HJE)
    c) Porcelain, and of continental manufacture, depicting a bust of Charles Edward Stuart.   (HJE, FCS)
    d) Silver
        1) engraved with a scene depicting a prospective Jacobite landing in Britain. Made in 1740 by Isaac Cookson of Newcastle.   (JSE)
        2) depicting King James VIII.   (WHM)
    e) Pottery, (Whieldon) depicting a portrait of the Prince in relief.   (ChC)
    f) Ivory
        1) anti-Jacobite and circa 1688, engraved with a satirical scene depicting James II with the three crowns falling from his head, the Pope, the Devil, and Louis XIV.   (ChC)
        2) Profile of Queen Clementina, in ebony frame.   (WC)
    g) Wax, depicting William Augustus, Duke of Cumberland.   (B)
    h) Unspecified, depicting two highlanders, with "PC" on their sporrans, and "Down with the rump" on their targes.   (SNE)

Plate
    a) Porcelain, with portraits of Rifleman Samuel Macpherson, & Piper Donald MacDonell of the Black Watch. Following the mutiny of 1743, Macpherson was one of three men executed, whilst Macdonell was transported to the colonies. 18th Century.
        (WHM, PCE, RMS, SC, NEA, CS3)

A Jacobite Legacy

b) Used by Charles while in a shepherd's hut on Raasay. (HJE)

c) Two, of china, part of a wedding present given by Lady Margaret Macdonald to Flora. (HJE)

d) Delft, from which Charles took oatcakes at a farmhouse near Forres, on his way to Culloden. (HJE)

e) Of English delftware, depicting the Boscobel oak supporting the crowns of the three kingdoms. (BM)

f) Pair, of English delftware, each decorated with an equestrian portrait of William, Duke of Cumberland, and bearing the legend: "Duke William For Ever, 1746". (PC)

g) English delft plate, decorated in manganese with an equestrian portrait of the Duke of Cumberland, with the date "1746", and the legend, in script: "Duke William For Ever". (B2)

Playing cards

These are the small playing cards used by Captain Felix O'Neill to keep a diary containing his account of the '45. (NLS)

Pocketbook

a) Worked by Flora Macdonald. (A)

b) Of leather, owned by Allan Macdonald of Kingsburgh, husband of Flora Macdonald, and has his name inscribed in gold lettering. (HJE)

c) Formerly belonging to Hugh Macdonald of Kingsburgh, stepfather to Flora Macdonald. (PC)

Pocket knife

a) Which belonged to Prince Charles Edward, and was given by him to a member of the Threipland family. (SNM)

b) With a brass handle, said to have belonged to Charles. (IM)

Pocket watch

a) Gold verge striking pocket watch by Conyers, London,

A Jacobite Legacy

with enamelled dial and outer case, formerly belonging to Alexander Irvine of Drum, who joined Charles at Edinburgh, and succeeded in escaping after Culloden. (NTS, DmC)

b) Silver verge pocket watch by Clark, London, the case back engraved with the scene of a kilted and bound Highlander being taken before an officer for interrogation. (CJS)

c) Belonging to Robert Forrester of Westerfrew Farm who safely guided the Prince and his army across the River Forth at the Fords of Frew, in 1746. (PC)

d) Made by Moore, London, in 1690, formerly belonging to Lord Lovat. (HJE)

e) Gold watch and seal formerly belonging to Flora Macdonald. (HJE, SNE)

f) Silver watch, with steel chain and seals, by Joseph Talby, taken at the battle of Falkirk. (HJE, GIE)

g) Gold and enamelled watch of French manufacture, belonging to Jean, wife of James Drummond, 2nd Duke of Perth, attainted 1716. She was imprisoned in Edinburgh Castle in 1746 for 9 months. It has a coral bead chain, and a coral seal and key attached. (SNM)

h) Gold and enamelled watch of massive dimensions, made by Robert Dingley, London. Attached to the watch are silver-gilt scissors, scissor-case, thimble and needle-cases, and an antique gold seal. Belonging to Jean, wife of the 2nd titular Duke of Perth, attainted 1716. (SNM)

i) Enamelled watch with portrait of James III on one side, and Prince Charles on the other, with a portrait of an unknown lady on the inside. (SNM)

j) Of silver, by Richard Vick, London, 1703, formerly belonging to James III, and left by him at Glamis Castle in 1716. (GC, SNE, GIE)

k) Of gold, formerly belonging to Bonnie Prince Charlie. It has a portrait of the Duchess of Albany in enamels on the back,

A Jacobite Legacy

surrounded by brilliants. The watch face is also circled with brilliants, and the hands are set with smaller diamonds. The maker was L'Épine of Paris, circa 1740. (TBM)

Point lace
    Belonging to Flora Macdonald. (HJE)

Porringer
    a) Silver porringer and cover belonging to Queen Clementina. (ERHS)
    b) Porringer of plain white pottery with triangular handle, used by the Prince whilst at the house of Mrs Lowry, Blackhall, during the siege of Carlisle in 1745. On a paper stuck to the base is written: "This cup, known by the name of Prince Charley's porridge cup, is the same that was used by the Young Pretender at Mr Lowry's, Blakewell, Nov. 1745. The siege of Carlisle." (THM)
Portfolio
    Belonging to Prince Charles Edward. (ERHS)

Portrait
    a) Needlework, of Prince Charles Edward Stuart. (CJS)
    b) Of painted carved wood, depicting Charles Edward Stuart. (PC)
    c) Wax portrait of King James VIII, by Isaac Goset. (WHM)

Portraits
    The student of the Jacobite movement has no shortage of images of the principal characters of the events of that era on which to focus his attention. Whilst many of these paintings have been carried out by some of the great portrait artists of the day, others are unsigned, and very often the description reads: "Artist unknown". The artist Francesco Trevisani painted well-known images of James III and his consort, Clementina, as well as of Mrs

A Jacobite Legacy

Marjorie Hay, wife of the Pretender's secretary, James Hay, and the cause of a major row between them, which resulted in Clementina seeking sanctuary in a convent. Trevisani also painted a portrait of Mrs Hay's brother, James Murray, the Jacobite Earl of Dunbar. The two young princes had their individual portraits painted in early childhood by Antonio David, and, in 1729, he executed two further portraits of the princes, wearing court dress, together with the Ribbons and Stars of the Order of the Garter. The latter are amongst the most popular images of the brothers, particularly that of Prince Charles, who, at the age of 9, is very distinctive in his scarlet and lace jacket. In the collection of Her Majesty the Queen, is a portrait of a 19 year old Charles by Louis Gabriel Blanchet, who, some years afterwards, painted a full-length portrait of Henry Benedict, resplendent in his cardinal's robes. James III was the subject of paintings by both Nicolas de Largillière and Domenico Dupra. The French artist Maurice Quentin de la Tour, who had produced excellent portraits of Louis XV and Marshall Saxe wearing armour, depicted Prince Charles Edward in similar garb in 1748, a likeness which was much copied by other artists. Louis Tocqué also employed this technique, as did Cosmo Alexander, in their own images of the Prince. Portraits of Charles Edward by Jean Étienne Liotard are amongst the best images of him, and like other well-known portraits, were much copied by other artists, to cope with the demand from England and Scotland amongst the Jacobite fraternity for images of their royal family. For the same reason, many of these portraits were reproduced in large numbers as engravings, which were then disseminated widely amongst their followers. An artist named Laurent Pêcheux, who painted Bonnie Prince Charlie at the age of 49, depicted him in armour, whilst the celebrated portrait of the Prince, painted 15 years later, was the work of Hugh Douglas Hamilton, who also painted a portrait of Charlotte, Duchess of Albany. Giles Hussey, an Irish artist living in Rome, painted other

A Jacobite Legacy

likenesses of Charles. Yet another portrait of the Prince was executed by the artist Joseph François Parrocel, and further portraits, of his father and grandfather, James III and James II, were painted by Hyacinthe Rigaud and Sir Godfrey Kneller respectively. Other well-known royal portraitists include Martin van Meytens and Anton Raphael Mengs. The French artist, François du Troy, painted very attractive portraits of Prince James and his sister, Princess Louisa, as children, whilst the former was painted in armour by Alexis Simon Belle, a favourite image of James which was widely reproduced. Portraits of other famous Jacobites, including young Lochiel, painted posthumously by Sir George Chalmers in 1762, Lord John Drummond, painted by Domenica Dupra, and Lord Elcho, possibly by the same artist, have all fortunately survived, along with many others, still in the possession of families having Jacobite ancestry. William Hogarth's sketch of Simon Fraser on the eve of his execution remains the enduring image of that duplicitous character. Flora Macdonald was famously painted by both Richard Wilson and Sir Allan Ramsay, the latter of whom also painted portraits of both Prince Charles Edward and Lady Mackintosh, the Jacobite "Colonel Anne". During the following century, many Victorian artists, including John Pettie and J B MacDonald, in accordance with the wave of sentimentalism current at that time, produced their own highly romanticised images of the Prince. On the Hanoverian side, portraits of the Duke of Cumberland and of the lairds of several of the "loyal" clans, including the Campbells, Macleods, and Macdonalds, are still to be found, sometimes in the castles of their descendents.

Pot

a) Cooking, of cast iron, standing on three legs. A brass plaque reads: "Cooking pot used by Prince Charlie when living in the cave at Glendo, Glenmoriston during August 1746."

(HJE, PC)

A Jacobite Legacy

b) Dutch oven, of red earthenware decorated with slip. Found on a rubbish tip at Ashbourne Hall, after the Prince's departure, together with the one below.   (DyM)

c) Posset, of slipware, from Ashbourne Hall, where the Prince stayed in December, 1745.   (DyM)

Powderhorns

These may be designated as Jacobite by virtue of having belonged to a known Jacobite, eg, that carried at Killiecrankie by Stewart of Ardshiel, or by Archibald Campbell at Culloden, or because of Jacobite symbolism incorporated in its decoration, eg, a rose within a snake, or references to Dunblane and Preston, etc. A further powderhorn bears the legend "Vivat Jacobus Tertius Magna Brittaniae Rex", (sic) whilst three more, one of large dimensions, were found on Culloden battlefield. One formerly belonging to Prince Charles is of French manufacture, preserved at Drumlanrig, and another, of carved ivory, was worn by him at a ball given in Holyrood Palace on the eve of the Battle of Prestonpans.   (WHM, CJS, DC, SNM, PC, HJE, BrC, GIE)

Prayerbook, Church of England

a) Formerly belonging to Isabella Lumisden, sister of Andrew Lumisden, who later became the Prince's secretary. She was an ardent Jacobite, who married Robert Strange, only after insisting on his joining the Prince's army. It is marked "Isabella Lumsden, 1747", and key words have been altered, "George" and "Frederick" becoming "James" and "Charles". (SNM, ERHS)

b) Prayerbook found by Lieutenant Ogilvy at the house of Macdonell of Glengarry in 1746, altered by erasure of the words "Frederick, Prince of Wales, the Princess of Wales", and the substitution of "Charles, Prince of Wales, Queen Clementina."

(BM)

A Jacobite Legacy

c) Formerly belonging to William Hynd, a soldier in Cumberland's army. (RMS)

d) Formerly belonging to Lord George Murray, and used by him in exile, in French. (BrC)

Printing plate

a) Of copper, showing the engraving by Nicholas Edelinck of Charles as a young boy, after David. The plate has been altered by the addition of a bonnet and cockade, probably by Robert Strange in 1745. (RMS)

b) For a satirical card commemorating the execution of Lord Lovat. (RMS)

Prints

a) Paper.
   1. Corporal Samuel Macpherson
   2. Corporal Malcolm Macpherson.
   3. Piper Macdonell.
   4. Private Farquar Shaw.
   5. Private Farquar Shaw, altered by the addition of a white cockade.

All four were deserters from the Black Watch in 1743. Samuel and Farquar were executed, the others transported. (HJE)

b) Silk

Showing Charles Edward Stuart in ordinary military dress, with cocked hat, mounted, and pointing with a baton towards a battle scene. By L Suruque. (BH, JSE)

Pulleyblock

a) Two, from HMS Dartmouth, which sank in Tobermory Bay in 1690. (RMS)

b) Fragments of pulleys from HMS Dartmouth. (RMS)

A Jacobite Legacy

Pulleywheel
   From HMS Dartmouth.   (RMS)
Punchbowl
   a) Of Chinese export porcelain, bearing the arms of the 2nd Duke of Argyll, who led the government forces at Sheriffmuir.
   (WHM)
   b) Adorned with the likenesses of a piper and rifleman of the Black Watch.   (FCS)
   c) Adorned with two enamelled portraits of Bonnie Prince Charlie.   (CJS)
   d) Adorned with a portrait of the Duke of Cumberland, and painted scenes from Culloden battlefield.   (PCE)
   e) Adorned with portraits of Bonnie Prince Charlie on the inside, and a piper and rifleman on the outside.   (PCE)
   f) Adorned with Chinese figures, said to be the one broken by the Prince whilst drinking with Macdonald of Kingsburgh on Skye.   (SNM, RMS)
   g) From Bannockburn House, and said to have been used by Prince Charles whilst a guest of Sir Hugh Paterson. (SAGM)
   h) Adorned with a medallion containing the words: "The Beggars Bennison", a Jacobite society based in Anstruther, Fife.
   (CS2)
   i) Decorated with an anti-Jacobite cartoon depicting a caricature of a highlander in a boghouse. The Scottish crown is shown falling down, and one inscription reads: "Nemo me Impune Lacessit", and another: "O Sawney why leave thou thy Nellie to moan?"   (RMS)
   j) Another similar.   (DsM)
   k) Of Jackfield ware.
   l) With portraits of Charles, and Jacobite symbols, and an inscription: "Old England-Uncovenent'd-Unportioned-Re-opened and Coloniz'd".   (WRS)

A Jacobite Legacy

2) Bearing 4 portraits of the Prince, between 7-petalled roses and buds. Used at the Cycle Club in Wrexham in 1710. (WRS)

3) Decorated in gold, with an inscription around the rim: "May all true gentlemen have a true steward, and may the tenant be ready when Steward comes". The bowl inscribed: "God Bless PC and Down with the Rump". (DH)

l) Lambeth delft punchbowl, circa 1745, adorned with a portrait of Charles after Sir Robert Strange. (ChC)

m) Chinese export punchbowl, circa 1770, bearing the arms of Argyll. Major-general John Campbell of Mamore was commander of the government forces in western Scotland during the Forty-Five, succeeding his cousin as 4th Duke, whilst his eldest son, Lieutenant-colonel John Campbell, served under Lord Loudoun, later to become 5th Duke. (CHG, G)

n) Decorated with portraits of the Duke of Cumberland, and scenes of Culloden battlefield. (WHM)

Purses

a) Richly decorated, and embroidered with the initials: "C P S". (SNM, ERHS, FCS)

b) Richly decorated, and embroidered with the initials: "J R S". (SNM, ERHS, FCS)

c) Said to be the Prince's, made by Flora Macdonald. (SNE)

d) Two, made from the timbers of the French frigate, La Fine, which brought Lord John Drummond to Scotland. The vessel went aground and broke her back in Montrose channel, following a sea chase. (PC)

e) Formerly the property of James Drummond, IVth Earl of Perth. (SNM)

f) Of brown leather, with a buttoned flap, formerly belonging to Rob Roy, together with a card detailing its history. (A)

A Jacobite Legacy

g) Of silk embroidered with gold thread, made by Princess Louisa, sister of James VIII. (CE)

Purse top
　　Portions of, found on Culloden field. (HJE)

* * * * *

Additional Notes: P

A Jacobite Legacy

A Jacobite Legacy

Q

Quaich
    a) Of fruitwood, with silver liner, engraved in Gaelic: "In remembrance of Dugael Cameron, Culloden, 16 April 1746."
    (AH, HJE)
    b) Of fruitwood, silver-mounted, a silver disc at the base inscribed: "God Bless King James The 8". This quaich is said to have been used by Prince Charles, and given by him to Ensign Home. (CE)
    c) Inscribed: "Prince Charlie 1745". (WHM)
    d) Formerly belonging to Flora Macdonald. (WHM)
    e) Silver-mounted, with plaque reading: "Welcome Charlie Stewart, Prestonpans, 21st September, 1745". (FCS)
    f) Wooden, formerly belonging to Prince Charles Edward, and used by him before and after Culloden. Presented by him to Donald Macgregor, House of Burn. (SNM, WHM, GIE)
    g) Of silver, from which Prince Charles drank whisky at Kingsburgh House. (HJE)
    h) and pepperpot, made by Hugh Macdonald, Stratherrick, whilst in hiding after the Battle of Culloden. (HJE)
    i) Found in the hand of the chief of the Magillivrays at Culloden. (HJE)
    j) Wooden, with a silver plaque in the base engraved with the Scottish crown, and inscribed: "God Save King James". Also marked "A.S.", and "Dec 21 1715". (SNM)
    k) Silver, used by the Prince the night he slept at Ruskie, in the inn occupied by Daniel Fisher. (SNM)
    l) Horn, found after the battle on Culloden field. (SNM)
    m) Two, of wood mounted with silver, having engraved loyal sentiments. (BrC)

A Jacobite Legacy

n) Wooden, with old contemporary print of the Prince, inset in the bottom, and covered with glass, out of which the Prince drank in Touch House, in 1745. (SNE)

o) Of laburnum wood with silver mounts, the handles engraved with the Scottish crown, and the Royal Cypher of James II. (NSA)

p) Of oak, bound by hoops in "coggie" style, and having a glass bottom and silver bands at both top and bottom. A 19th century inscription states that it was presented by the Prince in 1745 to Campbell of Kinloch. (A)

q) Of ebony and ivory, a silver plaque in the bowl engraved: "Timeo Danaos", a warning to Jacobites to guard their tongues. (RMS)

r) Of wood with silver handles, a silver plaque in the bowl engraved with a crown, JR, and 1692. (RMS)

* * * * *

Additional Notes: Q

A Jacobite Legacy

A Jacobite Legacy

R

Rapier
    a) Of French manufacture, carried by a highlander during the Forty-Five, and left by him at Chapel, in Lanark. (GIE)
    b) Left behind by King James VIII at Glamis Castle in 1716. (GIE)
    c) Said to have been formerly owned by Prince Charles. The blade is engraved with a thistle and crown,, and the cypher "CR", together with trophies of arms. (PC)

Rattle
    Used by Charles Edward as an infant. (GIE, SNE)

Razor
    and strop, silver-mounted, with Stewart crest, and coronet, said to have belonged to the Prince. (SNE)

Relief
    a) Ivory, of James II, by Roettier. The King is in profile, the crown on the back of his head. In the field is a reversed cornucopia, and the crown falling off a pedestal, with the inscription: "IACO II.....R" (JSE)
    b) Plaster, of the head of Charles Edward Stuart. (CDdM)

Reliquary   See also under Box
    a) Silver heart-shaped reliquary containing part of the pericardium of James II, in its original red silk bag, and engraved: "Reg Jac. Secundi Pericardium" around a crown. (ChC)
    b) Circular horn box reliquary containing the blood, hair, and garter ribbon of James II. (ChC)

A Jacobite Legacy

c) Box with tartan decoration, having a double lid with a secret portrait of the Prince, the inside in the form of a reliquary. Said to have belonged to Clementina Walkinshaw. (KM, SNM)

Ribbon,
  a) Garter
    1) Belonging to Prince James Francis Edward. (ERHS)
    2) Of blue silk, belonging to Prince Charles, with an old label reading: "Ribbon worn by Prince Charles Edward Stuart in the year 1745, given by him to Miss Barbara Stuart, and left by her to Charlotte Duchess of Richmond and Lennox, and left by Her Grace to Elizabeth, Duchess of Gordon". (BeC)
    3) Identical fragment given by the Prince to Lord Ogilvie. (CC)
    4) A piece of red silk Garter ribbon, mounted, with paste lettering, "HONI SOIT QUI MAL Y PENSE", together with a label reading "A piece of the ribbon of the garter worn by Prince Charles Stuart at the Battle of Culloden". Together with its paste buckle. (FCS, CJS)
    5) Piece of ribbon of the Garter belonging to Prince Charles. (ERHS)
    6) Garter and ribbon of the Order, belonging to Prince Charles. (ERHS)
    7) Piece of Garter ribbon worn by the Prince at Culloden. (ERHS, GIE)
    8) Garter and ribbon of the Order, belonging to Prince Charles, the Garter worked by the Countess of Derwentwater. (ERHS)
    9) Piece of ribbon of the Garter belonging to Prince Charles. (ERHS)
    10) Ribbon of the Garter belonging to Prince Charles. (SNM)
    11) Piece of Garter ribbon with lock of Charles' hair, set in a locket. (BrC)

A Jacobite Legacy

12) Piece of Charles' Garter ribbon. (BrC)
13) Piece of Garter ribbon of the Prince, worn by him at Culloden. (MeM)
14) Piece of the Garter ribbon worn by Charles, formerly belonging to Sir John Stanley. (JSE)
15) Length of the Prince's Garter ribbon. (RMS)

b) Jacobite

These were ribbons worn by Jacobite ladies in their hair, and were embroidered with a facsimile of the Prince carrying a targe and broadsword. Some found wearing these after Culloden had been fought were imprisoned overnight in Edinburgh Castle.
(PC, MeM)

c) Silk.

Long ribbon woven with the inscription: "O Cursed Rumps You Never Will Be Good, You Damn Your Souls With Spilling Harmless Blood." This was presumably worked in the aftermath of the butchery following the defeat at Culloden. (HP)

d) Tartan.

Small piece of silk tartan ribbon worn by Prince Charles.
(ERHS)

e) Thistle.

Piece of Prince James' ribbon of the Thistle. (ERHS)

Rigging crosspiece

From HMS Dartmouth. (RMS)

Rings

Several different types of ring have Jacobite associations. They might have been originally the property of Bonnie Prince Charlie, as in the case of a gold ring with gnostic gem, taken at Culloden, and another monogrammed "CPW", containing a lock of Charles' hair. Memorial rings to the Prince, and to members of the Jacobite aristocracy, including Lord Lovat, and Lord George

A Jacobite Legacy

and Lady Amelia Murray, are also known, as well as others commemorating the executed Jacobite peers. Six rings associated with Flora Macdonald are amongst those listed. Hair rings generally contain a lock of hair belonging to one or other member of the Stuart royal family, in a glazed compartment, often with an inscription at the back. Portrait rings are also found, painted in enamels, and James is the subject of two such rings, the first whilst still a prince, the second, a memorial ring issued after his death. Yet another portrait ring contains a miniature in ivory of Bonnie Prince Charlie, and is said to have been worn by him, while another carries a profile of his head, after Giles Hussey. The wedding ring of Charles and Louise, bearing appropriate inscriptions, has also survived. Another type of enamelled ring which is believed to have been popular, is in the form of a white rose, symbol of Jacobitism since 1688. Other rings may have been presented as gifts to certain individuals, including Clementina Wharton, Mrs Samuel Ward of Derby, and Beatrice Jenkinson, to whom he presented a fabulous rose diamond, surrounded by four smaller ones. Another type of ring is the seal ring, used by Jacobites to seal their clandestine letters to one another. These usually incorporated a Jacobite symbol, such as a rose or forget-me-not, together with a Jacobite slogan, usually in Latin, such as "Fiat", "Redi", "Reddite", "Ab Obice Major", etc., but sometimes in English, "Follow Me", "Dinna Forget", "Forget Me Not", etc. Other Jacobite rings have similar slogans, but are not seal rings, since the image is not reversed.

(RMS, IM, WHM, PC)

1) Hair ring, containing lock of Bonnie Prince Charlie's hair, removed in 1744, with an inscription in French beneath.   (PC)

2) Memorial ring to executed Jacobite peers.   (RMS)

3) Gold ring gifted by the Prince to Clementina Wharton. A large crown surmounts two heart-shaped stones, amethyst and garnet, each surrounded by brilliants.   (IM)

4) Ring consisting of one large diamond, surrounded by 10

A Jacobite Legacy

smaller ones, presented by the Prince to Mrs Samuel Ward of Derby. It was at her house that Charles and his officers took their meals, the Prince's food being always first tasted by her son. The ring, his own, was presented on his departure. (DyM)

5) Seal ring, of gold and hardstone, engraved with a rose and single bud, and "Turno Tempus Erit". (PC)

6) Seal ring, of gold and bloodstone, engraved "Ibo". (PC)

7) Jacobite gold bloodstone ring, "Awa Whigs Awa". (ERHS, GIE, FCS)

8) Jacobite silver bloodstone ring, "Awa Whigs Awa". (SNM, ERHS, FCS)

9) Memorial ring to Lord George Murray. (CJS)

10) Memorial ring to Lady Amelia Murray. (CJS)

11) Gold and diamond memorial ring to Prince Charles. (CJS)

12) Memorial ring to Lord Lovat. (RMS)

13) Glove ring of gold set with an agate, belonging to Flora Macdonald. (ERHS)

14) Wedding ring of Flora Macdonald. (ERHS, HJE)

15) Gold ring with gnostic gem, belonging to Bonnie Prince Charlie, taken at Culloden. (ERHS)

16) Gold hair ring, containing a lock of the Prince's hair. (ERHS)

17) Portrait ring bearing a likeness of Prince James. (ERHS)

18) Gold memorial ring with enamelled portrait of King James VIII. (ERHS)

19) Gold ring given by the Prince to a member of the Graham family. (ERHS)

20) Gold ring with monogram "CPW" and a lock of Charles' hair. (ERHS)

21) Diamond ring given to Beatrice Jenkinson. (ERHS)

22) Gold ring with miniature in ivory of Prince Charles, and said to have been worn by him. (SNM, ERHS)

23) Gold memorial ring to executed Jacobites. (PC)

A Jacobite Legacy

24) Gold seal ring, of moss agate engraved with a rose and single bud, the shoulders engraved with roses, with acanthus on the loop. (PC)

25) Ring given by King James VIII to John Cameron of Fassifern. (HJE)

26) Marquise ring, worn by Flora Macdonald in memory of a son, Ranald, "Lost in the Ville of Paris". (A stricken vessel) (HJE, SNE)

27) Silver ring with bloodstone, "The Rose That's Like The Snaw". (SNM, ERHS, GIE, FCS)

28) Silver ring, "Do Come". (SNM, ERHS, GIE, FCS)

29) Gold hair ring, containing a lock of Prince Charles' hair. (SNM)

30) Gold hair ring, containing a lock of Charles' hair. (TBM)

31) Diamond ring, belonging to William Boyd, Earl of Kilmarnock, executed 18 August 1746. He gave this ring, together with the one described below, to Reverend Laurence Hill, minister of Kilmarnock. There is a large central diamond, surrounded by 10 smaller ones, and 3 smaller on each shoulder. (SNM, SNE)

32) Emerald ring, formerly belonging to the Earl of Kilmarnock, and given before death to Reverend Hill. (SNM)

33) Enamelled ring, inscribed: "Pro Rege at Patria", the motto of the Edinburgh Jacobite society, the Royal Oak Club. (SNM)

34) Hair ring, with lock of Charles' hair, inscribed: "Got from Gask". (BrC)

35) Gold ring with lock of Charles' hair under crystal, engraved "Love and Honour", with Prince of Wales' feathers, and a thistle and rose, said to have been presented by Charles to Flora. (CDhM)

36) Memorial ring to Lady Amelia Murray, with lock of her hair. (Another) (BrC)

37) Memorial ring to Lord George Murray. (Another) (BrC)

38) Gold memorial ring containing lock of Charles' hair and an inscription. (PC)

A Jacobite Legacy

39) Gold seal ring, engraved with a dolphin, the emblem of the Society of Sea Serjeants, inscribed on the underside: "Success to the Society". Each shoulder is in the form of a butterfly with a rose beneath, both symbols much used by the Jacobites. (PC)

40) Ruby ring brought by James II from England, later belonged to Cardinal York, and now part of the Scottish Regalia. It had been owned formerly by Charles I, and was traditionally used at the coronation of all Stuart kings. (SNE)

41) Wedding ring of Charles and Louise of Stolberg, consisting of an oval turquoise, engraved with a crown, and surrounded by brilliants. This opens to reveal a portrait of Charles. On the outside is engraved: "By evry claim 'tis yours", and has the initials of both, as well as the date of the nuptials, 17 April, 1772. (PC)

42) Gold ring with profile portrait of Charles, after Hussey. (PC)

43) Memorial ring containing a lock of Viscount Dundee's hair, with the letters "VD" worked in gold, surmounted by a coronet. Inside the ring is engraved a death's head, and "Great Dundie for god and me J Rex." (SNE)

44) Ring adorned with a miniature of the Prince. (SNE)

45) Marquise ring, of blue enamel, containing a lock of the Prince's hair. (SNE)

46) Ring, with a miniature of Henry, Duke of York. (SNE)

47) Gold and enamel lozenge-shaped ring, with crown and cipher: "C.R." (SNE)

48) Gold ring given by Charles to a member of the Jacobite Wilson family in 1745. (SNE)

49) Diamond ring containing a lock of Charles' hair. (WRS)

50) Memorial ring of James III. The face bears the white rose in green and white enamel, and "Jacobus.....Gratia", under crystal. On the curved guard of gold and black enamel, a Latin inscription reads: "James III ....died in exile", together with the date of his death. (WRS)

A Jacobite Legacy

51) Gold ring, with miniature portraits of James and Clementina. (WRS)

52) Ruby and diamond ring in the form of the Order of the Garter surmounted by a Royal crown, and on the loop in blue enamel: "Dieu et mon Droit". It was sent by the Prince to Sir Watkin Williams Wynn, and was presumably intended as a temporary substitute for the genuine article. (WRS)

53) Gold memorial ring containing a plait of hair under crystal, inscribed in the loop: "Flora Macdonald in Memoriam". (PC)

54) Gold ring with large amethyst belonging to the Prince, and presented by him to John Farquarson of Allargue in 1750. (IM)

55) Rings with bezels containing miniatures of the Old Pretender. (BM)

56) Gold and enamel ring with an inscription commemorating the execution of the Jacobite Lords Balmerino, Kilmarnock, Derwentwater, and Lovat, as well as 17 officers of the highland army, in 1746 and 1747. (BM)

57) Ring containing strands of Charles' and Flora's hair. (IM)

58) Gold, with a crowned JR under crystal. Given to Sir Peter Halkett of Pitfirrane by James VII, when he fled London. In its original red velvet purse. (RMS)

59) Cameo ring with a portrait of Charles, inscibed: "CPR" and "Dum Spirat Spero". (RMS)

60) Ring inscribed: "CPR 1745 Dum Spirat Spero". (RMS)

61) Silver signet ring with paste setting, and a bust of the Duke of Cumberland, inscribed: "WD of Cumberland". Found near Inverness. (RMS)

62) Ring containing a portrait of Lady Katherine Gordon, whose husband became the 7th Earl of Wemyss. (JSE)

63) Memorial ring in enamel on gold, said to have been made by the Jacobite goldsmith, Ebenezer Oliphant, to commemorate the 4 executed peers. (JSE)

A Jacobite Legacy

64) Gold ring containing a plaited lock of Charles' hair, engraved: "Prince Charles Edward Stuart's Hair 1746". (TBM)

65) Gold ring containing the plaited hair of Charles Edward Stuart. (CE)

66) Gold ring of pointed oval shape, containing plaited hair under crystal, said to be that of Charles and Flora Macdonald, surrounded by seed pearls. (IM)

67) Gold portrait ring depicting Prince James, on ivory. (GIE)

68) Gold ring worn by Prince Charles Edward, containing miniatures of James and his sister Louisa. (GIE)

69) Gold seal ring set with a lapis lazuli, engraved with a thistle, and the words: "Dinna Forget". (PC)

70) Gold ring with cameo of Prince Charles Edward, Inscribed "CR III 1766". (ChC)

71) Miniature ring of Charles I, formerly belonging to the Old Pretender. (GIE)

72) Miniature ring of Charles II, formerly belonging to the Old Pretender. This ring and the previous one, were gifted by him in 1715 to Alexander Gordon of Auchentoul. (GIE)

73) Memorial ring, engraved in the loop: "Donald Mcdonald (sic) of Kinlochmoidart, suffered October 18, 1746, for King and Country", and containing a lock of his plaited hair under crystal. (CDdM)

Ring sundial
Carried by the Lord President, Duncan Forbes of Culloden. (HJE)

Rock
From taken from Cluny's cave. (MnM)

Rolls
Being small rolls of paper used to convey secret dispatches, and concealed in the curls of wigs or in the spur-holes of boots. See also under Box. (SNM)

A Jacobite Legacy

Ruffles

Lace, said to have been given by the Prince in lieu of wages, together with a lace collar and a handkerchief purported to be stained with the tears of Charlotte, his daughter.   (WHM)

* * * * *

Additional Notes: R

A Jacobite Legacy

A Jacobite Legacy

S

Saddle
    Belonging to Prince Charles Edward.   (SNM)

Saddlebag
    A portion of Lord George Murray's saddlebag.   (WHM)

Sampler
    a) Dated March 1746, together with "April 16 1746", and "At Culloden Muer Peter Law".   (CE)
    b) Dated 1729, worked by Isabel Lumisden, sister of Andrew Lumisden, the Prince's secretary, and wife of the engraver, Sir Robert Strange.   (SNM)

Sash
    a) Of white silk, belonging to Prince Charles Edward, and taken with his baggage after Culloden.   (ERHS, GIE, WHM)
    b) Mounted section of sash worn by Prince Charles, with a letter signed by Flora Macdonald, reading: "Fragment of the Sash of Prince Charles Edward Stuart. Given to me by Mrs. Watson Beliot of Bishophall Watson whose great uncle was private secretary to King James and who got the whole of the sash and many other relics".   (ERHS)
    c) Tartan sash belonging to Flora Macdonald, and presented by her to a family member in 1780.   (RH)

Sauceboat
    Silver, formerly belonging to Flora Macdonald. (NCDCR)

Scarf
    Piece of scarf worn by Bonnie Prince Charlie at Edinburgh, in 1745.   (MH)

A Jacobite Legacy

Scent bottle
  a) Engraved with Jacobite emblems.   (ChC)
  b) Formerly belonging to Flora Macdonald.   (PC)

Seals
   These were used by the Jacobites to impress the wax sealing their clandestine letters. There were three main types of seal, plain, ring, and watch fob seals. They were usually gold, having an agate, bloodstone, carnelian, or similar insert, which was engraved with a Jacobite symbol in reverse, often incorporating some form of Jacobite slogan. Symbols include flowers, similar to those engraved on Jacobite glass, usually the rose or forget-me-not, sometimes with a thistle in addition, the text in Latin, and of necessity a short one, often "Fiat", "Redi", or "Reddite", and sometimes in English, as in "Awa Whigs Awa", "Dinna Forget", or "No Union". One seal to have survived is Bonnie Prince Charlie's personal one, emblazoned with his coat of arms, and the legend: "Charles III by the Grace of God King of Great Britain, France and Ireland". The great seal of Henry IX is another which is still extant.
  a) Plain
    1) 12 unmounted seals, with their impressions, showing various Jacobite devices.   (WRS)
    2) Gold, with large carnelian bearing a portrait of the Prince in highland dress, facing to his right, after Sir Robert Strange. The seal surmounted by a crown.   (PC)
    3) White agate and silver, personal seal of Charles III. (CJS)
    4) Gold seal of Charles III and Louise of Stolberg.   (IM)
    5) Steel seal of the Jacobite Earls of Winton.   (GIE)
  b) Ring
    1) Hardstone, engraved with a rose, and the legend; "Turno Tempus Erit".   (PC)
    2) Bloodstone, engraved "Ibo".   (PC)
    3) Agate, engraved with forget-me-not, and "Dinna Forget".   (PC)

A Jacobite Legacy

      4) Agate, engraved with a rose, having a single bud. (PC)
      5) Glass, with the head of Charles, and the initials: "PC".
   (WRS)
      6) Gold, with red carnelian, bearing Charles' head, with the Crown and Garter. (WRS)
      7) Carnelian, showing the arms of Stuart of Traquair, with its bear supporters. (TH)
      8) Citrine, with the arms of Lord Traquair. (TH)
      9) Topaz, with the arms of Lord Traquair. (TH)
  c) Watch fob
      1) Agate, engraved with a forget-me-not, and the words: "Forget me not". (PC)
      2) Agate, engraved "Awa Whigs Awa". (PC)
      3) Engraved "No Union". (PC)
      4) Engraved "Redi". (PC)
      5) Engraved "Reddite". (PC)
      6) Engraved "Dinna Forget". (PC)
      7) Topaz, engraved "Me Sequeo".(sic) (PC)
      8) Agate, engraved with Prince of Wales' feathers and "Fingask Castle ". (FCS)
      9) Agate, engraved "Dinna Forget". (CJS)
      10) Moss agate, engraved "Follow Me". (PC)
      11) Topaz, engraved with a rose and thistle on the same stem, and Redii". (PC)
      12) With an impression of the Prince in highland dress. (BrC)
      13) Glass, with portrait of the Prince after Hamilton. (PC)
      14) Glass, bearing the head of Charles. (HP)
      15) Agate, bearing the motto of the Stuarts of Traquair, "Judge Nought", and a Jacobite rose with a single bud. (PC)
      16) Lapis lazuli, bearing a thistle, and the words: "Dinna Forget". (PC)
  d) State
      1) Three, which belong to the period when the 4th Marquess of Tweeddale was Secretary of State for Scotland. (JSE)

A Jacobite Legacy

2) Great seal of Henry IX, of cut steel, showing his name and titles, and his Royal Arms surmounted by a cardinal's hat.
(ChC)

Serviettes
Twelve, of coloured damask, from Gortleg House. (HJE)

Shaving bowl
Of silver, engraved with the arms of Prince Henry Benedict, Cardinal York. (GS)

Shirt
a) Piece of, belonging to Charles Radcliffe, Lord Derwentwater, executed 1746, and allegedly stained with his blood.
(RS)
b) Another. (EDC)

Shirt frill
Made of lace, which was left at Fassifern by the Prince.
(SNM, ERHS, GIE)

Shirt studs
Of silver and pebble, worn by Bonnie Prince Charlie, contained in a box whose gold lid is engraved with the figure of a highlander. (SNM, ERHS, GIE)

Shoes
Pair of shoes belonging to Charles, and given by him to Flora Macdonald in 1746. (SNM, GIE)

Skean dhu
With bone handle, reputed to have belonged to Henry Patullo, muster-master of Charles Edward Stuart's army. (KM)

144

A Jacobite Legacy

Sleeve links
 a) Silver sleeve links, engraved "C P W", for Charles, Prince of Wales. (ERHS)
 b) Pair, given by the Prince to Cameron of Lochiel in Paris, in 1747. (HJE, SNE)
 c) Of agate and silver, taken from James Sandilands, Master of Torphichen, who fought on the government side, and was seriously wounded at Prestonpans. (RMS)
 d) Two engraved gold sleeve links, said to have been given by the Prince to Flora Macdonald during his flight. (ChC)

Slippers
 Pair, belonging to Flora Macdonald. (SNE)

Snuff bottle
 Spar snuff bottle gifted to Murray of Broughton by the Prince. (ERHS)

Snuffbox
 1) Of tortoiseshell covered with striped paper, of French manufacture, with miniature of Bonnie Prince Charlie as a youth, set in the lid. (PC)
 2) Of tortoiseshell mounted with silver, the lid interior containing a portrait of the Prince after Sir Robert Strange. (PC)
 3) Enamelled, in Stuart tartan, with hinged double lid concealing a hidden portrait of the Prince. (PC)
 4) Of silver, belonging to Flora Macdonald. The initials of herself and husband are engraved on it, "A. M'D., F. M'D." (SNM, ERHS, HJE)
 5) French, with portrait in the lid of Bonnie Prince Charlie. (ERHS)
 6) Of tortoiseshell, containing a medal commemorating the escape of Clementina from Innsbruck. (ERHS)
 7) Of imitation tortoiseshell, with a portrait of the Prince. (ERHS)

A Jacobite Legacy

8) Of tortoiseshell, presented by the Prince to Hay of Restalrig. (ERHS)

9) Of silver, oval-shaped, the lid inset with a portrait miniature of the Old Pretender, with Boscobel House below. (ERHS)

10) Of tortoiseshell and silver, heart-shaped, and "JR/8" inlaid in silver. Belonging formerly to the Radcliffe family. (ERHS)

11) Of silver, double-lidded, with concealed portrait of Prince James, and given by him to his physician, Dr Kenyon. (ERHS)

12) Of ivory, the lid having a portrait miniature of the Prince, formerly belonging to Murray of Broughton. (ERHS)

13) Of gold and tortoiseshell, with a portrait of the Prince concealed behind a moveable mask. (ERHS)

14) Another, of gold and tortoiseshell, with a portrait in the lid of Bonnie Prince Charlie. (ERHS)

15) Of tortoiseshell and silver, presented by the Prince to Lady Mary Menzies, after Culloden. (ERHS)

16) Of gold, containing a secret portrait of the Prince. (ERHS)

17) Of gold, presented by the Prince to Donald Macdonell of Lochgarry. (ERHS, GIE)

18) Of gold, containing a portrait of Marie Leczynska, wife of Louis XV, and formerly belonging to the Prince. (ERHS, HJE)

19) Of silver, the lid engraved with Jacobite symbols, containing a secret compartment inside the lid, similarly engraved and chased, depicting an allegorical scene of a dog devouring the bones of the enemy. Dutch. (PC)

20) Of silver, engraved with the coat of arms of Cameron of Lochiel. Given by the Prince to Lochiel in Paris in 1747, and engraved: "snuff box or dram cup while skulking in ye Highlands". Marked "PCS". (HJE, AH)

21) Of wood, containing 8 tunic buttons found at Culloden. (GS)

22) 17th century, with the Royal insignia in the lid, and an oval plaque inscribed: "This box belonged to James the Pretender". (GS)

A Jacobite Legacy

23) Of enamelled tortoiseshell and silver, the lid inlaid in silver with the figures of a highlander and his lady, with butterfly and floral decoration, formerly belonging to James Francis Edward. (TH)

24) Of petrified wood, heart-shaped, containing a hardstone cameo of a dog, the rim set with rubies, with a diamond thumbpiece, and concealed portrait of Prince Charles. (FCS)

25) Of tortoiseshell and silver, engraved with a crowned thistle and rose, and containing a concealed portrait of Bonnie Prince Charlie. (GM)

26) Of mother of pearl, formerly belonging to Simon Fraser, Lord Lovat. (HJE)

27) With double lid, containing a portrait of Bonnie Prince Charlie, formerly belonging to Lord Lovat. (HJE)

28) Japanned circular snuffbox, with miniature of the Prince. (HJE, SNE)

29) Of gold and porcelain, with an enamelled portrait of the Prince on the outer side of the lid, and containing the ribbon which he wore in his bonnet, and a gold proof impression of an intended victory medal. (HJE)

30) Taken from the body of an officer, Charles Fraser, killed at Culloden. (HJE)

31) With false lid, concealing a portrait of James Francis Edward in armour, wearing the Ribbon of the Garter. (SNM)

32) Of silver, presented by Bonnie Prince Charlie to Angus Macdonald of Borrodale, in whose house the Prince spent the first and last days of his stay in Scotland. Inscribed: "Testimonium grati animi", with an additional inscription added by Sir Walter Scott detailing its history. (SNM, TBM)

33) In Stuart tartan, the lid bearing a portrait of Charles in harlequin dress, carrying a sword and targe, given by him to Archibald Stewart, Lord Provost of Edinburgh. (BrC)

34) Of silver, belonging to Charles, engraved: "Carolus Inter Reges ut Lillium Inter Flores". (BrC)

A Jacobite Legacy

35) Of silver, with Jacobite symbols on the lid. (BrC)
36) Formerly the property of the Marquis of Tullibardine. (BrC)
37) Of tortoiseshell, said to have belonged to the Prince. (SNE)
38) Of silver and ivory, belonging to the Jacobite, John Byrom of Manchester, having the Byrom arms at its base. (MJE)
39) With concealed portrait of the Prince. (MJE)
40) Painted, with concealed portrait of the Prince. (MJE)
41) Of horn and pinchbeck, with concealed portrait of the Prince. (WRS)
42) Of horn and pinchbeck, with concealed portrait of the Prince. (Another) (WRS)
43) Of French enamel, with concealed portrait of the Prince. (WRS, PC)
44) Used by the Prince after Culloden, and presented by him to Donald M'Rae. (SNE)
45) Of horn and pinchbeck, with a false lid bearing a likeness of the Prince. (WRS)
46) Of horn and pinchbeck, bearing a portrait of the Prince, and believed to have been used at meetings of the Cycle Club. (WRS)
47) Of tortoiseshell, double lidded, the inner lid with the likeness of the Duke of Cumberland, painted by Christian Friedrich Fricke. Presented to Lieutenant-Colonel George Howard, who commanded the 3rd Foot at Culloden. (NAM)
48) Gold, with lid and base of agate, the inner lid engraved: "Awa Whigs Awa". (PC)
49) Of silver and mother-of-pearl, with a likeness of Prince Charles. (IM)
50) With a miniature of Charles beneath the lid. (RMS)
51) Gold-mounted tortoiseshell, with a depiction of James VIII in relief on the lid, said to have been given by the Prince to Flora Macdonald. (RMS)

A Jacobite Legacy

52) Gold-mounted tortoiseshell, set with a miniature of Charles on the lid. (RMS)

53) Gold, with a hidden portrait of Charles. (RMS)

54) Made from part of a thorn tree, near which Colonel Gardiner was killed on 21st September 1745, and so inscribed. (RMS)

55) The lid painted with a full-length portrait of Charles in highland dress. (JSE)

56) Of ivory, the lid with a silver plaque engraved with a crown and "JR". Inside the lid is a plumbago portrait of Prince James Francis Edward, inscribed at the side with: "This is He". (JSE)

57) Gold, with latticework design, said to have been presented by the Prince to Lord Provost Aird Smith of Glasgow. (JSE)

58) Silver, the lid engraved: "Be not given to changes, fear God and honor the King", and, "Alexander McGruther", who made it while in Newgate prison. The base inscribed: "17th July 1717". (JSE)

59) Silver, containing a portrait of Lady Katherine Gordon set in the lid. She was the wife of Francis Charteris, and is said to have served the Prince refreshments outside Prestonhall, after the battle of Prestonpans. (JSE)

60) Of silver and mother-of-pearl, with a portrait of Charles inside the lid. (IM)

61) Of Liverpool enamel, circa 1760, the base painted with flowers, the lid bearing a portrait of Prince Charles Edward in armour, after Quentin de la Tour, a star in the background. (PNB)

62) Of metal, the detachable lid bearing a likeness of the Prince within an engraved brass cartouche. (HM)

63) Of staghorn mounted with silver, and engraved with a crown and thistles, with the later inscription: "Prince Charles Edward Stuart", engraved under the crown. (PC)

A Jacobite Legacy

64) Of papier maché, the lid bearing a portrait of the Prince in campaign dress, wielding a sword. (BH)
65) Silver snuffbox, with a tortoiseshell lid inlaid with a silver "Retreat to Scotland" medal. (WHM)
66) Metal snuffbox, with a bronze "Retreat to Scotland" medal inserted on its lid. (WHM)
67) Tortoiseshell snuffbox formerly belonging to Duncan Cameron, who fought at Culloden. (WHM)
68) Tortoiseshell snuffbox, its lid inlaid with a glass "highlander" portrait of Charles. (WHM)

Snuffmull

The distinction between these and the above is not at all clear. Whatever the material used in their construction, gold, silver, ivory, tortoiseshell, etc., boxes could be used for many different purposes, and the problem is probably merely an etymological one. The practice adopted here is to adhere to the original description.

a) Of horn, having silver mounts with engraved crest and motto of the Ogilvie clan. (CC)
b) Of coquilla shell and ivory, the lid inlaid in silver, "James III", and a small plaque at the front states that it was formerly the property of James III. (PC)
c) Of tortoiseshell and mother-of-pearl, formerly belonging to Duncan Cameron, who fought at Prestonpans. (WHM)
d) Of ivory, with silver inlay, engraved "IR 8", and the names of Marr, Ormond, and Sobiesky.(sic) (ERHS, GM)
e) Of ivory, formerly belonging to James III. (ERHS)
f) Presented by Bonnie Prince Charlie to Maxwell of Kirkconnell. (ERHS)
g) Of horn, and silver-mounted, formerly belonging to Sir John Maclean of Duart, who was "out" in the Rising of 1715, and later owned by his son, Sir Hector Maclean, who was imprisoned in Edinburgh Castle during the Forty-Five. (DtC)

A Jacobite Legacy

h) With pestle, used by Cluny Macpherson during his 9 years in hiding. The iron hoop surrounding it was made and attached by himself. (SNM, GIE)

i) Jacobite snuffmull, with silver mounts inscribed "Tempora Mutantur et Nos Mutamur in Illis", and "A.S., 1751." (PC)

j) Of Scottish provincial silver, by Hugh Ross of Tain. Oval capstan form, the hinged, slightly domed lid chased with scallop shell and scrolling foliage. The base engraved: "William Munro of Achanie his Box 1744". Munro fought at Culloden on the Hanoverian side, sustaining wounds from which he died 2 years later. (CS1)

k) Of ebony and ivory, silver-mounted, with plaque engraved: "AS", direct and reversed, and the date "1743". On the silver rim: "Post Nubila Phabus" (sic) Alexr Smith 1745 Longmay". The inscription signifies "Sunshine after clouds", a reference to the hoped-for restoration of the Stuarts. (PC)

l) Of horn and ivory, silver-mounted, and engraved: "Pro Rege et Patria". (The motto of the Royal Oak Society.) (BrC)

m) Of ivory, and large dimensions, formerly belonging to I Robertson of Lude. (BrC)

n) Of ivory, with silver lid engraved with the crest, motto, and armorial shield of Hamilton of Bangour. (PC)

o) Presented by James II to the Kirkconnell family. (SNE)

p) Of horn, and octagonal cylindrical form, the silver top engraved with the arms of Buchanan. An inscription on a silver rib reads: "A gift from a friend to William Buchanan of Kirenoch". The silver base is engraved with a crowned thistle, and the initials: "IR VIII". (C&E)

q) Of horn, said to have been made in a house on Culloden Moor by a survivor of the battle. (MM)

r) Of horn, engraved: "To Scotland No Union God Save King James Ye VIII". (MM)

s) Of horn and silver, the top engraved "1745". The body

A Jacobite Legacy

inscribed: "John Morison". Below is the Morison crest, with the motto: "Uno Ictu". John Morison of Bognie, Banffshire, was taken after Culloden. His subsequent fate is unknown, but he later returned to Scotland, and succeeded to the estates of Bognie, Mountblairy, Cobairdy, and Frendraught. The acquisition of the Frendraught titles is indicated by the presence of a Viscount's coronet. (PC)

t) Of horn, formerly belonging to William Forbes of Blackton, who was "out" in 1715, engraved: "Reviresco". (MM)

u) Of horn and silver, the top engraved with the arms of Lord Traquair. (TH)

v) Given by the Prince to Donald Macdonald of Scothouse, killed at Culloden, 1746. (CDdM)

Spectacles

a) Belonging to Donald Macleod of Galtrigal, Skye, (Gualtergil), the Prince's boatman and pilot, who became known as "the faithful Palinurus". (DnC)

b) Formerly belonging to Henry, Cardinal York, in their original Italian leather case. (ChC)

Sporran

a) Of brass and leather, found on Culloden battlefield. (BrC)

b) Of silver-mounted sealskin, with silver tassels, worn by Bonnie Prince Charlie. (SNM, ERHS, HJE, SNE, GIE)

c) Sporran which belonged to Bonnie Prince Charlie. (ERHS)

d) Sporran reputedly belonging to Rob Roy. (A)

e) Sporran reputedly belonging to Rob Roy. (Another) (IC)

f) Sporran worn by Malcolm Fraser of Abernethy at Culloden. (HJE)

g) Sporran worn at Culloden by Donald Macdonald. (HJE)

h) Sporran of sealskin, left by the Prince at Stonehouse, in the hamlet of Moorhouse, near Carlisle, together with a pistol of French manufacture. (PC)

A Jacobite Legacy

Sporran top
    a) Reputedly formerly belonging to Rob Roy. (HJE, SS)
    b) Brass, worn at Culloden by Peter Reid, brewer, of Montrose. (HJE)
    c) Worn by Robertson of Woodsheal at Culloden, top only original. (CDhM)

Spur
    a) Pair of silver spurs belonging to Prince James. (ERHS)
    b) Brass spur found at Culloden. (RMS)
    c) Pair of silver spurs belonging to Prince Henry Benedict. (ERHS)
    d) Iron spur found at Culloden. (PC)
    e) Silver spur said to have been worn at Culloden by the Prince or one of his attendants. (HJE)
    f) Pair of spurs belonging to Simon Fraser of Lovat. (HJE)
    g) Pair of steel spurs worn by Prince Charles, and given by him to Laurence Oliphant the Elder, of Gask. (SNM, GIE)

Standard
    On June 14 1746, witnessed by a large crowd, fourteen standards captured at Culloden, including that of the Prince, were ceremoniously burnt at the Mercat Cross in Edinburgh by the public hangman, assisted by the chimney sweeps of the city. Later in the same month other Jacobite standards were burnt publicly at the cross. However, several standards did survive, including the banner of Clan Chattan, dramatically rescued after Culloden by a Mackintosh clansman, as well as the banners of the Stewarts of Appin, Camerons of Lochiel, and Ogilvy's Forfarshire Regiment. The Macpherson banner also survived, the clan arriving only after the battle had ended.
    a) Macpherson banner. (MeM)
    b) Banner of the Stewarts of Appin. (HJE, RMS)

A Jacobite Legacy

c) Banner of the Ogilvy's Forfarshire Regiment. (DuM)
d) Cameron banner. (AH)
e) Portion of Bonnie Prince Charlie's banner. (ERHS)
f) Macdonald banner, said to have been carried on the Prince's triumphal entry to Edinburgh. (RH)
g) Cameronian standard, of straw-coloured silk, with thistle and crown decoration, and the words: "Nemo Me Impune Lacesset", and the date: "1689". (SNM)

Standard holder
Of silver, belonging to the Stewarts of Appin. (IBH, WHM)

Star of Garter
Belonging to Prince Charles Edward. (ERHS, GIE, SNE)

Statuette
a) Of Bonnie Prince Charlie, in bronze. (HJE)
b) Lead statuette by Sir Henry Cheere, of the Duke of Cumberland in equestrian pose. (NAM)

Stick
Of blackthorn, said to have belonged to the prince. (CDdM)

Stickpin (jabot pin)
a) With heart-shaped glazed panel containing a lock of Charles Edward Stuart's hair, surmounted by a crown. (CJS)
b) Of gold, with enamelled top, depicting Bonnie Prince Charlie, aged about 14. (PC)
c) Of gold set with rubies, and "CP" in script, containing a lock of the Prince's hair. (IM)

Stone
From the floor of Cluny's cage. (WHM)

A Jacobite Legacy

Stool
 a) Having three legs, and bearing a brass plaque inscribed: "This stool was sat on by Prince C.E. Stuart while under hiding in the Isle of Skye, 1746". (PC)
 b) Upon which the Prince sat while in hiding on South Uist after Culloden. (SNM)

Streamers
 Worn by Jacobite ladies during the Forty-Five. See also Jacobite ribbon. (ERHS)

Suit
  Richly embroidered with silver thread, belonging to the Jacobite, Basil Hamilton of Baldoon, who was "out" in 1715, and eulogised in verse after his death by William Hamilton of Bangour. (SNE)

Sundial
 and compass, of silver, a relic of the Stuarts, belonging to Lord Lovat. (HJE)

Sword-liner
 Of red velvet lined with buff leather, cut off by the Prince from his sword hilt, and presented by him as a souvenir to the sisters of Robert Anderson of Whitburgh, who guided the highland army through the bog at Prestonpans. It was later acquired by Robert Chambers, and attached by Robert Forbes to the front board of Vol III of The Lyon in Mourning. (NLS)

Swords
 Several swords reputed to have been found on the battlefield of Culloden are known. Generally, these are basket-hilted broadswords, having two sharpened edges, but some are backswords, having only one sharp edge, and were used by the

A Jacobite Legacy

cavalry. Moy Hall has examples of each of these varieties. The sword carried during the battle by the Duke of Perth was one of the Scottish National Memorials exhibited at Bishop's Castle, Glasgow, in 1888. Swords used at the Battles of Killiecrankie, Falkirk, and Prestonpans, have also been exhibited at this and other exhibitions. Bonnie Prince Charlie's sword, with chased silver basket hilt, decorated with trophies of arms and a medusa's head, matching that on the Warwick Castle targe, is currently on display at the Culloden Exhibition, and is a wonderful example of a basket-hilted broadsword. It is traditionally believed to have been found with the Prince's baggage after Culloden. Donald Cameron of Lochiel's silver-hilted sword, preserved at Achnacarry House, is also of this type. The sword of the Marquis of Tullibardine, the Jacobite Duke of Atholl, who was one of the Seven Men of Moidart, is a very fine example of a broadsword with gilt basket hilt, whilst in complete contrast is the military backsword of Donald Fraser, the heroic blacksmith of Moy, whose plain hilt is simply constructed of sheet metal. The swords of Alexander Macdonald of Keppoch, who met his fate at Culloden, and William Boyd, Earl of Kilmarnock, who was executed at Tower Hill on June 9 1746, have both survived, as has that of John Graham of Claverhouse, Viscount Dundee. Quintessentially Jacobite, is the group known as "Prosperity to Scotland" swords. These are so called because the blades are engraved with the words: "Prosperity to Scotland and No Union", whilst, on the other side, the inscription reads: "God Bless King James VIII." These swords were made in the early years of the 18th century, following the Act of Union of 1707. Many other swords with Jacobite associations are in existence, despite the severe penalties imposed by the Disarming Act of 1746 for concealment of such weapons, but perhaps the most intriguing is a sword preserved at the West Highland Museum, the repository of a large number of Jacobite artefacts, which was discovered in 1880 in a cave on the shores of Loch Treig, still gripped by the

A Jacobite Legacy

bones of an arm and hand, and evoking painful and powerful images of the tragic events of the times.

Swordstick
   Said to have been used by James Graham, Viscount Dundee.
                                                         (RMS)

* * * * *

Additional Notes: S

A Jacobite Legacy

A Jacobite Legacy

T

Table
a) Traditionally reputed to have been used by William, Duke of Cumberland, on which to sign death warrants after the Battle of Culloden. (DMAG)
b) Kitchen-table, from Culloden House. (HJE)
c) Table, used by the Prince on his visit to Gask in 1745. (PC)

Table cover
a) Of embroidered linen, belonging to Prince Charles. (ERHS, HJE)
b) Made of flax spun by Flora Macdonald. (ERHS)

Tablets
Of Princess Louise of Stollberg. (ERHS)

Table napkin
Used by Bonnie Prince Charlie when at the house of Macdonald of Kingsburgh in Skye. (ERHS)

Tankard
Silver, engraved with Culloden battle scenes, and known as the Cumberland tankard. By the London goldsmith, Gabriel Sleath. (NAM)

Taperstand
Pair, constructed of brass, belonging to Prince James Francis Edward. (ERHS)

Tapestries
a) Four tapestries taken from original paintings of scenes set in the 1745 rebellion, depicting Bonnie Prince Charlie and others. (CJS)

A Jacobite Legacy

b) Contemporary tapestry depicting the Duke of Cumberland on horseback, with a redcoat apprehending a figure in highland dress, representing the Prince.   (LT1)

Targe
These will be designated as Jacobite by virtue of their former ownership by known Jacobites. Probably the most famous of these are the two silver-mounted targes, almost certainly of French manufacture, which were gifted to the two young princes by James Drummond, Duke of Perth, as accoutrements of highland dress. Both are richly inlaid with trophies of arms, consisting of drums, flags, shields, pistols, and swords, and have central bosses in the form of a medusa's head. One of these is in Warwick Castle, whilst the second, which came into the possession of Cluny Macpherson after Culloden, is now in the collection of the Royal Museum of Scotland. A matching sword to the Warwick Castle targe, is preserved at Brodie Castle in Invernessshire. Another famous targe is that belonging to Colonel John Roy Stuart, which can be seen at Marischal Museum, Aberdeen, and is reputed to have been left by him at Lowther Hall on his retreat from Derby. The targe of the gentle Lochiel, pierced by three musket balls, is in the possession of his descendants at Achnacarry House, whilst that owned by Small of Dirnanean is on display at Blair Castle. Tullie House Museum in Carlisle has another targe, decorated with brass nails in the form of crowns and thistles, which is reputed to have been used at Culloden. A brass-mounted targe used by one of the Grants of Glenmoriston during the Rising of 1719 is in a private collection, whilst many other targes, either privately owned, or in museum collections, have by tradition been used by the Jacobite army during the Risings of 1715 and 1745.

Tartan,
Pieces of,   (See also Cloak, Coat, Jacket, Plaid, Trews)

A Jacobite Legacy

a) A piece of hard tartan, measuring 9" x 4", traditionally from the Prince's clothing. (BeC)

b) A piece of hard tartan from Culloden. (WHM)

c) A piece of tartan from Bonnie Prince Charlie's clothing. (WHM)

d) Mounted piece of Bonnie Prince Charlie's trews. (CJS)

e) Fragment of Drummond tartan worn by Charles at Holyrood. (RMS)

f) Framed fragment of tartan formerly belonging to the Maxwells of Terregles, said to be a portion of the Prince's plaid. (RMS)

g) Fragment of tartan from a kilt worn by the Prince in 1746. (RMS)

h) Fragment of tartan from the Prince's clothing, with an accompanying letter of authentication. (SE)

i) Piece of Stuart tartan cut from the hangings of a bed slept in by the Prince. (GIE)

j) Pieces of tartan from the cloth and lining respectively, of the waistcoat given by Macdonald of Kingsburgh to the Prince, and later exchanged by him with that of Captain Malcolm Macleod. The latter hid it in the cleft of a rock, and, after his release from confinement in 1747, returned to the spot, but found only these fragments remaining. They are attached to the back board of Vol III of The Lyon in Mourning. (NLS)

k) Two pieces of tartan inset into the boards of an 1827 copy of Robert Chambers' History of the Rebellion in Scotland in 1745. Inscribed in pencil within are the words: "This tartan is a piece of Prince Charlie's kilt which was left at Crammond Farm when Mr Stuart hid him there". (SE2)

l) Mounted piece of tartan with documentation affirming that it was worn by Fraser of Altyre at Culloden. (B3)

A Jacobite Legacy

Tea caddy
Constructed from the timbers of La Fine, raised in 1875. (MeM)

Teapot
a) china, used by Bonnie Prince Charlie while having tea with Provost George Bell of Conheath, near Glencaple, in December, 1745. (DsM)
b) china, decorated with oak leaves and acorns, and the figure of Prince Charles. 18th century. (DC)
c) from which Prince Charles drank tea, on the evening of his arrival at Gortleg House, after Culloden. (HJE)
d) silver, belonging to Flora Macdonald. (HJE)
e) used by George Seton, fifth Earl of Winton, while confined in the Tower in 1716. (SNM)
f) saltglaze and blue enamel, decorated with a white rose, oak leaves, and "CR III". (MJE)
g) silver bullet teapot by William Aytoun of Edinburgh, 1740, engraved with the arms of James Campbell of Auchinbreck, father-in-law to Donald Cameron of Lochiel. (PC)
h) Staffordshire salt-glazed stoneware teapot, enamelled in blue and white, and decorated with a rose and "Charles III". (BM)

Thimble
Gold, enamelled, and set with emeralds, belonging to Lady Jean Gordon. (GIE)

Tiles
Dutch tiles taken from the fireplace of a room in the house in Derby Old Market, where the Prince held his last council meeting before the retreat to Scotland. (ChC)

A Jacobite Legacy

Tobacco box

Of brass, used by John Ogilvy of the Quick, Cortachy, Forfarshire, who was Ensign in Lord Ogilvy's regiment, and fought at Culloden. (HJE)

Toddy ladles

a) Two, made of wood, with carved handles, from Gortleg House. (HJE)
b) Reputed to have belonged to Prince Charles. (HJE)
c) Three, of silver, reputed to have belonged to Charles. (EDC)

Token

a) In white glass, depicting the head of James III, the likeness being that on the medal issued by Ottone Hamerani for the proxy wedding of James and Clementina in 1719, when James Murray stood proxy for the Old Pretender. (PC) See also medallion.
b) Jacobite, unspecified, 1719. (HJE)
c) In the form of a mourning buckle for John, Marquis of Tullibardine, killed at Malplaquet in 1709, and sent as a token by his brother, the then Marquis, to Robertson of Faskally in 1715. (BrC)

Tooth

Canine tooth, said to have been lost by the Prince in infancy, mounted on silk, in an ivory frame. (WHM)

Tray

Silver, inscribed: "F McD", formerly belonging to Flora Macdonald, with accompanying silver jug, sauceboat and ladle, and left by her in North Carolina on her departure in 1778. (NCDCR)

Tree,

a) Portion of, from Moy. (MnM)
b) A piece of the thorn tree under which the Prince is said to have stood at the Battle of Prestonpans, (WHM)

A Jacobite Legacy

Trews
    Tartan, belonging to Prince Charles. (WHM)

Tumbler
    a) French silver tumbler, engraved with the arms of Ogilvy, which was carried by Lord Ogilvie at the Battle of Culloden. (PC)
    b) Glass, out of which Charles drank, in a farmhouse at Cranston, Midlothian, on his retreat from England. (HJE)
    c) Venetian glass, formerly belonging to Louise of Stolberg, Charles' Queen. (WRS)

* * * * *

Additional Notes: T

A Jacobite Legacy

A Jacobite Legacy

U

* * * * *

V

Valances

Pair, from a set of wall hangings, embroidered in wool and silk, on linen. In the centre, "IRCR 1719", surmounted by a crown. Sunflowers, roses, and oak leaves are all depicted. Made to celebrate the marriage of James and Clementina.   (RMS)

Vestments

Belonging to Prince Henry Benedict, brother to Prince Charles Edward.   (FC)

* * * * *

A Jacobite Legacy

W

Waistcoat
  a) Of embroidered silk, belonging to Prince Charles and given by him to his doctor at Rome. (IBH, WHM)
  b) Of white embroidery, having gold buttons, worn by the Prince at Holyrood Palace, and given by him to James Stirling of Craigbarnet. (HJE, SNE)
  c) Worn by Prince Charles, and afterwards belonging to the descendants of Flora Macdonald. (HJE, SNE)
  d) Two, of embroidered silk, worn by William Maxwell of Kirkconnel, son of the 5th Earl of Nithsdale, both of whom were enlisted in the Prince's army. (DsM)

Walking reins
  Belonging to the infant James VI. (SNM)

Walking stick
  Belonging to Macdonald of Kinlochmoidart. (WHM)

Wallet
  a) Of silver, belonging to the Stewarts of Appin. (WHM)
  b) Of leather, inscribed: "The Prince his own book 1748". (RS)

War-scythe
  One of 100 supplied to the citizens of Dumfries for defence of the town during the rebellion of 1715. They were issued to a certain number of "Sythmen" in every company, to be employed at the "Barricades and Trenches". (SNM, GIE)

Watchcase
  Jewelled, and of gold filigree, presented by King James to Lady Threipland in 1716. (ERHS)

A Jacobite Legacy

Watchchain
   Of gold, belonging to Prince Charles, and exchanged by him for that of James Gordon of Cobairdy, in Paris in 1747.
(SNM, HP)

Watchpaper
   Roundel bearing the names of Jacobites who gave their lives for the cause in 1745, with central inscription: " 75 Sufd for Royal Virt, 1746", made to be inserted in the back of watches, partly in order to protect the winder holes. (PC)

Watchstand
   Made from the wood of a walnut tree which was planted by Prince Charles Edward at Dean's farm, near Bathgate. (WHM)

Whip handle
   Of wood, its covering woven and strung, and decorated in red, white and blue. An old handwritten label reads: "Whip which belonged to Prince Charles, 1745." (FCS)

Whisky bottle
   a) From which the Prince drank a dram at the Battle of Culloden. (HJE)
   b) Of pocket size, belonging to Rob Roy, and presented by him to a clansman in Balquhidder. (SNE)

Whistle
   a) of wood, left by the Prince's army at Broadstone Hill farm, Stockport, on its departure. (DyM)
   b) of bone, with silver top, which belonged to Viscount Dundee. (SNM)

A Jacobite Legacy

Wig
 Belonging to Bonnie Prince Charlie. (ERHS)

Will
 a) Of Charles Edward Stuart. (NAF)
 b) Of Henry Benedict Stuart. (RSAR)

Windowseat
 From Fassifern, home of the "gentle" Lochiel's brother, John, embroidered with a white rose. (WHM)

Wine-taster
 Of silver, said to have been presented by Charles to William Keith, Earl Marischal. (WRS)

Wood,
 a) Block of, from the wreck of the French frigate La Fine. (MeM)
 b) Piece of wood taken from the eight-oared boat used by the Prince during his escape, and later attached by Robert Forbes to the board of Volume IV of The Lyon in Mourning. A second piece is now missing. (NLS)

Writing-desk,
 Portable, from Gorthleg House, possibly used by Charles to write his letter of farewell to the chiefs. (PC, CE)

* * * * *

A Jacobite Legacy

Additional Notes: W

A Jacobite Legacy

X

* * * * *

Y

* * * * *

Z

* * * * *

A Jacobite Legacy

It was the purchase, several years ago, of a "Highlander" portrait of Prince Charles Edward Stuart, after Sir Robert Strange, which first led me into the magic world of Jacobite memorabilia. I had long been interested in, and fascinated by, Scottish history. This in itself had begun in my earliest years, but had become rekindled during my researches amongst primary source material for my book on the Scottish pistol. The miniature in question had been exhibited at the Exhibition of the Royal House of Stuart, held in the New Gallery, Regent Street, London, in 1889. This inevitably led to a search for the catalogue of the said exhibition, and of other such catalogues, most of which are not easy to find. I soon became aware that many of the items on display at one exhibition of Jacobite memorabilia, were quite often duplicated at another, whilst contrarily, a large number of objects exhibited at one, have never reappeared at another. As will be seen from the present work, objects having possible Jacobite significance are numerous as well as diverse, both in character and type. There are a great many examples of locks of the Prince's hair, or of Jacobite snuff mulls or boxes, hair rings, and pieces of the Prince's tartan, but until now, there has been no attempt made to define these artefacts, or to list specifically the objects themselves, so that the Jacobite enthusiast is quite unaware of the number, or indeed, the nature, of these surviving articles of our historic past. By trying to include the bulk of such catalogues as described, as well as encompassing as many items displayed in local museums and in private collections as was reasonably possible, a list of Jacobite memorabilia has thus been compiled. The sources of these articles are listed separately, under "KEY". Items appearing at more than one source are labelled accordingly. In cataloguing the individual locks of Charles' hair, great care was taken that these were not duplicated, and similar precautions were taken with such frequently recurring items as

A Jacobite Legacy

pieces of the Prince's tartan, and with the snuff boxes referred to above. Inevitably, a catalogue of this type can never be complete. No-one could in a single lifetime visit every museum and private collection. Many such collections exist, and are known only to a few friends and family members. It is for this reason that pages have been left at the end of each letter of the alphabet, in order that the interested reader may add other objects which appear to differ from those already listed. Indeed, the author would welcome all such information with gratitude, and the publishers will gladly relay any such information. In no way do I claim particular expertise on the subject of Jacobite memorabilia. My object was merely to compile a catalogue for enthusiasts such as myself, to make our study and collecting easier and, to some extent, more rewarding. Our chosen subject is a fascinating one, and my sole aim is to make it even more so, by attempting to delineate its full extent. Hopefully, the reader may make his or her own contribution to the existing knowledge.

Martin Kelvin.

A Jacobite Legacy
Captions for pictures

Gold and agate snuffbox

Interior of upper lid, with the popular Jacobite slogan, "Awa Whigs Awa".

Parcel gilt belt buckle, gifted by the Prince to Ian Dubh Mackinnon of Mackinnon. The supporters, a lion and leopard, are unique to the chief of Clan Mackinnon. The reverse is inscribed: "Carolus Princeps Deo Patriae Tibi".

Brass and carnelian seal, with a likeness of the Prince.

Wax impression (after Sir Robert Strange)

Watch fob seal of gold and hawk's-eye agate, showing a rose and single bud, symbolising King James VIII and Prince Charles Edward Stuart, with, above, the motto of the Stuarts of Traquair, "Judge Nought".

Portrait of Prince Charles Edward after Hussey, circa 1750.

Jacobite medals, 1712-88.

Anti-Jacobite medals, 1717-46.

Miniature of James Francis Edward Stuart, the Old Pretender, after Alexis Simon Belle, 1712.

Snuffmull of ivory and silver, bearing the arms and motto of the distinguished Jacobite poet, William Hamilton of Bangour.

Snuffmull of ivory and ebony, belonging to the Jacobite, Alexander Smith of Longmay, dated 1745. The inscription reads: "Post Nubila Phabus",(sic), literally, "Sunshine After Clouds", a reference to the hoped-for restoration of the Stuarts.

Lid, showing inscription.

Jacobite powderhorn dated 1716, with engraved decoration including the words: "Vivat Jacobus Tertius Magna Brittaniae Rex" (sic) ie.,

"Long live James III, King of Great Britain".

Engraving by Hogarth of Miss Jennie Cameron of Glendessary.

Engraving of the Battle of Culloden, 16 April 1746, by Laurie and Whittle, 1797.

Engraving by Nicholas Edelinck of David's portrait of Charles at the age of 6, altered by Strange in 1745 by the addition of a bonnet and white cockade.